The Impoverished Spirit in Contemporary Japan

The Impoverished Spirit in Contemporary Japan

Selected Essays of Honda Katsuichi

Edited by John Lie

Translated by Eri Fujieda,
Masayuki Hamazaki, and John Lie

Monthly Review Press
New York

Library of Congress Cataloging-in-Publication Data
Honda, Katsuichi, 1933–
   The impoverished spirit in contemporary Japan: selected essays of Honda
Katsuichi/edited by John Lie; translated by John Lie, Eri Fujieda, and Masayuki
Hamazaki.
      p.   cm.
   ISBN 0-85345-858-8 (cloth): $34.00.—ISBN 0-85345-859-6 (pbk.): $16.00
   1. Japan—Politics and government—1945- 2. Japan—Intellectual life—1945–
I. Lie, John. II. Title.
DS889.H55   1993
952.14—dc20   93-28331
                                                               CIP

Monthly Review Press
122 West 27th Street
New York, NY 10001

Manufactured in the United States of America
10   9   8   7   6   5   4   3   2   1

To my friends
at the Kawasaki Peace Information Centre,
especially Uemura Hideaki
and Tenymô Ako

Contents

Introduction:
Honda Katsuichi
and Political and Intellectual Life
in Postwar Japan

A 1987 survey of Japanese college students showed that Honda Katsuichi was the author they were "most interested in reading."[1] Until his retirement in 1992, Honda was a star investigative reporter for the prestigious Japanese daily Asahi Shinbun. Since 1974, most of his essays have been published in the thirty-volume series The Impoverished Spirit; in addition, there are over twenty titles in the Honda Katsuichi series published by Asahi Shinbunsha. Large bookstores in Japan feature Honda "corners" where his bestsellers, ranging from travelogues to a manual for writers, are on display. It is difficult to invoke a comparable figure in the United States or the United Kingdom. Honda shares some of the concerns and styles of Alexander Cockburn, Paul Foot, and I. F. Stone, yet no one would expect American college students to name a hard-hitting, progressive journalist as the author they are "most interested in reading."

In this introductory essay, I want to locate Honda's work as a journalist in the context of postwar Japan, while previewing the major topics of this collection of essays. Honda underwent a major transformation after the Vietnam war. His earlier writings, which were inspired by youthful enthusiasm for adventure and science, were quasi-anthropological investigations of nonindustrial peoples. It was his celebrated and courageous coverage of war-torn Vietnamese villages that not only made him famous but politicized him. His interests became involuted; his writings focused on the corruption and complacency of Japanese life.

Postwar Japan and the Two Establishments

Let me first offer a thumbnail sketch of Japanese political and intellectual development from the end of World War II until the mid-1960s. For the purposes of this essay, I will highlight the political dominance of the right and the intellectual dominance of the left.

Emperor Hirohito's surrender to the Allies on August 15, 1945, ended Japanese military aggression, which had continued without pause since the invasion of Manchuria in 1931. The U.S.-led occupation force proceeded to transform Japan from a military power into a peaceful country. Progressive legislation attempted to purge feudal and fascist elements from Japanese life. Prewar thought-control and press censorship ended overnight, unleashing critical writings and political activities. There was therefore a remarkable rejuvenation of leftist and labor movements immediately after the war.

However, by the late 1940s the U.S. occupation force had reversed its progressive policy; Japan's projected role shifted from being the "Switzerland of Asia" to being the "factory of the Far East." East Asia became a major site of the Cold War: the "fall" of China and the Korean war firmly positioned Japan as the bulwark against international Communism in the minds of U.S. policymakers. The occupation force therefore sought to stem increasingly militant labor and leftist movements, and the right enjoyed a resurgence, soon becoming the dominant political force in Japan.[2] Major politicians who were associated with prewar militarism and nationalism and who had been purged from political life were resurrected. Many of them assumed key roles in Japanese politics. Perhaps the most egregious rehabilitation was that of Kishi Nobusuke, a Class A war criminal, who served as prime minister in the late 1950s.[3] Prewar militarist and anti-American politicians became the core of a new group of conservative politicians who pledged unswerving allegiance to the United States. With the change in foreign policy, the guiding ideology became economic growth. This technocratic orientation is exemplified by Ikeda Hayato, prime minister in the early 1960s and one of the architects of postwar economic growth.[4]

The conservative coalition has governed uninterruptedly since the amalgamation of the two conservative parties into the Liberal Democratic Party (LDP) in 1955. Neither liberal, nor democratic, nor a party, the LDP as an organization is dedicated to the control of the Diet (the Japanese parliament) through a number of interpenetrating and overlapping personal networks whose currency is campaign finance.[4]

Against the conservative dominance of parliamentary politics, the left has remained divided into myriad parties and factions. The two main left-wing parties in the postwar period have been the Communist Party and the Socialist Party.

Although united in their criticism of the dominant LDP, the two have remained divided over many issues.[5] Nevertheless the left dominated the cultural and intellectual sphere in the early postwar years. Partly because it was the sole organization to consistently oppose prewar Japanese militarism, the Communist Party, with its Marxist ideology, was influential among labor movements and intellectuals. Most intellectuals were anti-militarist and hence anti-LDP. In effect, the left establishment was composed of graduates of Tokyo University and other elite universities who went on to work at elite cultural institutions. For example, Iwanami Shoten and *Asahi Shinbun*, which represented, respectively, the pinnacles of publishing and journalism, were dominated by progressive forces and ideologies. Until the 1970s, very few university professors were affiliated with LDP politicians, *Asahi Shinbun* remained associated with progressive editorials, and Iwanami Shoten published Marxist and progressive novels, criticisms, and academic works.

It is in this context—the political dominance of the right, the intellectual dominance of the left—that Honda entered public life. But first, let us examine his earlier career.

Honda as an Outsider: Science and Adventure as Vocation

Honda's early writings reflected his youthful interests in adventure and science. They were therefore of little concern to the mainline political and intellectual debates.

After finishing high school in his native Shinshû,[6] Honda studied pharmacy at Chiba University and then enrolled in a graduate program in genetics at Kyoto University. Mountain-eering, an enthusiasm he first acquired in high school, was his major interest in college. For example, he seriously contem-plated climbing Mount Everest before Sir Edmund Hillary had done so.[7] His travels took him to the Himalayas, and his first book, published when he was twenty-six, was *The Unknown Himalaya*. In the same year, 1958, he began to work as a staff writer for *Asahi Shinbun*.

This sense of adventure dominates Honda's early writings. Indeed, he first attained national prominence in 1963 by covering the largest mountaineering accident to date in Japan. Partly as a reward for his scoop, he was able to satisfy his thirst for adventure by traveling to Canada to report on the Inuit. His report was serialized in *Asahi Shinbun* later that year and won wide acclaim and popularity. The dispatches were col-lected in *Canada, Eskimo*, which became a bestseller. The book was one of the first long-term investigative reporting projects in Japanese journalism.

Honda was one of the pioneers of the ethnographic method, which entails participation and observation, in Jap-anese journalism. Honda followed his foray into Canada with reports on the New Guinea Highlanders and the Bedouins of the Middle East. The trilogy of travel and adventure writings firmly established his reputation as a star reporter of *Asahi Shinbun*.

His empathetic mode of reporting combined a keen appre-ciation of his physical surroundings with the ability to grasp vivid details of social life. These documentary reports are, however, devoid of the political or social criticism that would mark his later writings. Indeed, they belong more properly to the genre of adventure and naturalism.[8]

Why did Honda's anthropological adventures become bestsellers in Japan? In the period of prewar Japanese colonial expansion, writing about far-away lands and peoples had become popular. The hunger for colonial encounters with preindustrial peoples, however, had not been satisfied because of the Japanese defeat, postwar poverty, and restrictions on overseas travels. Honda's reports from distant parts of the globe fulfilled an interest that was widely cultivated but unattainable for the majority of Japanese in the early 1960s.

Honda's interest in the natural world and science dates back to his childhood. In a later reminiscence, Honda cites Jean-Henri Fabre's *Entomological Souvenirs* as the most influential book of his youth.[9] The nineteenth-century French entomologist's careful and objective description of the insect world was a popular book for Japanese children. *Entomological Souvenirs* developed in Honda a deep respect for the natural world, as well as the useful journalistic skill of close and objective observation. Further, the elegant Japanese translation of Fabre's work by a renowned Europhile, Hayashi Tatsuo, was to have an impact on Honda's prose style.

Honda's nascent scientific interest led to his graduate studies in genetics at Kyoto University. Although he ultimately abandoned a scientific career, his brief sojourn in academia brought him into contact with renowned Japanese naturalists, including Imanishi Kinji and Umesao Tadao, who practiced and advocated a humanistic and ethnographic approach to biology in the tradition of Fabre and Darwin. Honda also gained an abiding respect and concern for logic and rational argumentation—the basis of his blunt empiricism. Aside from sharpening his descriptive and analytical skills, Umesao in particular influenced his writing style.

The Vietnam War and the Politicization of Honda

The Vietnam war politicized Honda and laid the foundation for the concerns he pursued in the 1970s and 1980s.

In one sense, Honda's decision to report on the Vietnam
war was an obvious extension of his prior work, which involved firsthand visits to foreign sites: the plunge into the
battlefields of Vietnam can be seen as a continuation of his
search for adventure. Further, *Asahi Shinbun*'s decision to
dispatch one of its star reporters was well-calculated. With the
mounting Japanese interest in the escalating war, there was
stiff competition for scoops among the leading dailies. This
conjuncture of personal and corporate interests led Honda to
the wartorn villages of Vietnam.

Honda's ethnographic approach served him well. He spent
countless hours observing and listening to the Vietnamese
peasants. He wrote empathetically about the lives of these
people who were not dramatically different from the villagers
of his youth. At the same time, he was shocked by the savagery
of the U.S. soldiers' racism toward the Vietnamese people. In
coming to an "anthropological" understanding of Vietnamese peasants, Honda differed from U.S. journalists and soldiers who remained largely indifferent to their lot. As Marilyn
Young remarks: "A Japanese reporter, Katsuichi Honda, understood the distance between American soldiers and the
ordinary scenes of Vietnamese rural life they witnessed daily
without ever comprehending."[10]

Honda was one of several Japanese reporters who gained
worldwide admiration for their courageous reporting from
Vietnam, shunning the safe routines of the military briefing
sessions.[11] Honda's reporting from Vietnam rode the wave of

anti-Vietnam war sentiment in Japan. Newspaper accounts had a tremendous impact on the Japanese public, and the overall tenor of the reporting was critical of the United States. In this sense, Honda's reporting was in the mainstream of 1960s Japanese political and intellectual opinion. To be sure, the pro-American LDP was solidly behind U.S. intervention in Vietnam, but the majority of Japanese were opposed to the fighting in general and to U.S. bombings in particular.[12] Furthermore, intellectuals were nearly unanimous in condemning the U.S. role.

Honda's Vietnam coverage made him a hero to progressive Japanese, including both the left establishment and the new left and citizens' movements represented by Beheiren, a grass-roots anti-Vietnam war group. His five-month-long series, "War and People," in *Asahi Shinbun* won wide acclaim and became a long-running bestseller when published as *The Villages of War* in 1968. Its impact can be gauged by the fact that it was translated into English in the same year under the title *Vietnam: A Voice from the Villages*, and 50,000 copies were sent to the United States and elsewhere.[13] The translation and distribution were carried out largely through the efforts of Beheiren.

Honda saw the Vietnam war as a war of invasion—"the latest in a series of invasionary wars perpetrated by the United States":

> Why Indian wars? American soldiers called Filipinos "gooks" and did not regard them as human beings. . . . In the Korean war, Koreans were called "gooks" and considered inhuman. Because they are not human beings, it is all right to kill them like insects or slugs. The American attitude toward Native Americans, which did not change for over a century, was applied to Asians.[14]

Honda made many trips to Indochina and continued to write about the problems and prospects for Vietnam and Cambodia into the 1980s. In 1978 and 1980, he tracked the fate of the Pol Pot regime in Cambodia, focusing on its genocidal policy. Two of his works, *Journey to Cambodia* and *Verifying the Cambodian Massacre*, published in 1981 and 1989 respectively, investigated and verified the massive and inhumane killing by the Khmer Rouge.

Writing Against Racism and Colonialism

Honda's involvement in the Vietnam war opened new vistas. An immediate offshoot was his investigation of the United States waging a savage war on its own turf. Hence, in 1969 he traveled around the United States, lived in Harlem, New York, and visited various Native American reservations. His primary concern during his half-year sojourn was to examine racism, which he believed underlay some of the ferocity of U.S. killing of Vietnamese peasants.

The United States that Honda found was wracked by racial conflicts and violence. The result of his glimpse, published as *The United States of America* in 1970, offered a sharply revisionist account of a country that was widely regarded as an ideal society in Japan. Inner-city poverty and violence and the shoddy treatment of the indigenous peoples combined with the image of the U.S. military presence in Vietnam to produce an unflattering portrait of a society in turmoil.

Honda's reporting on the United States marked several departures from his earlier work. Most obviously, it was his first extended coverage of a major industrial country. More important, however, is the significance of what the Japanese call *mondai ishiki*, or "problem consciousness," which can be understood roughly as heightened political awareness and consciousness. Thus whereas Honda's previous reports on indigenous peoples, such as the Inuit of Canada, had focused on their daily life and physical environment, political concerns came to the foreground in his writing on the United States, including his coverage of Native Americans.

Honda became increasingly critical of ethnography or any kind of reporting that ignored political context and power relations. He criticized his teacher Imanishi for failing to challenge the establishment. As he wrote in 1970 on the closing of the Exploration Club (which he had helped to found in 1956 while he was a student at Kyoto University): "Without political awareness ('problem consciousness') our materials will be used for evil rather than for good."[15] In effect, he rejected many of his earlier assumptions and methods. The Vietnam war had taught him that without an understanding of power relations—without "problem consciousness"— seemingly neutral reporting can be used by the powers-that-be to further oppress their victims. Ultimately Honda became critical of his earlier enchantment with adventure and "colonial" anthropology.

In the 1970s and 1980s, Honda continued to travel widely and report from the third world. His new political consciousness dominated these travels and investigations. For example, in 1987 and 1988, when he retraced Magellan's route around the globe, he treated the voyage as a European invasion of the non-European world. In *Magellan Came!*, published in 1989, he focused on the negative repercussions of Magellan's and later Europeans' "discovery" of the native peoples of Asia and the Americas. Similarly, his 1989 trip to Australia was no ordinary ethnography of the lives of the aborigines, but a report of their plights and struggles from their perspective.

A consistent theme in Honda's post-Vietnam war writings is a critique of U.S., and more broadly Western, imperialism and the racist attitude that underlies it. Those groups that are discriminated against, whether African Americans or Native Americans, are the ultimate victims of the European invasion of North America, and their ancestors cannot be viewed merely as self-contained groups of "primitive" peoples. The indictment of racism and colonialism as an invasion, then, marks much of his writings on the native peoples around the world.

Honda's attention gradually focused on similar groups of people within Japan, particularly the Ainu of Hokkaido, and he wrote a series of articles on their history and culture, beginning in the 1970s. The Ainu people are one of the native peoples of *Ainu-moshiri*, the Ainu term for present-day Hokkaido. The ethnic Japanese, or inland people (*Naichijin* in Japanese; *Shisamo* or *Shamo* in Ainu), gradually encroached on and incorporated Hokkaido, which is one of the four main islands of the Japanese archipelago.[16] In one of Honda's first political pieces on the Ainu, he surveyed the situation of the indigenous peoples of the United States, Vietnam, and elsewhere and then came to the following conclusion: "In the end, our task is to be concerned not with the situation of other countries but rather with that of Japan, which is right here and which we must attempt to change by our efforts."[17]

The Ainu are for him a paradigmatic instance of an exploited, victimized people. In this sense, they are to Japan what Native Americans are to the United States, and he excoriates Japan's past and present racism no less than that of the United States.

To understand the significance of Honda's articles on the Ainu, it is crucial to note that central to Japanese self-definition is the belief that Japan is a racially and ethnically homogeneous society. This is a belief that is widely shared not only in Japan but abroad as well, and has been invoked to account for a variety of Japanese characteristics, ranging from phenomenal economic success and group orientation to insularity and xenophobia.

Japan is, however, neither homogeneous or monoethnic. The process of Japanese nation-building entailed the incorporation of other ethnic and cultural groups. This was the case of Hokkaido, which had its distinct language and tradition, as well as Okinawa. More recently, as a result of Japanese colonial expansion in the first half of the twentieth century, many Koreans and Chinese migrated either voluntarily or by force into the Japanese archipelago. By 1945, the Korean population in Japan had swollen to well over 2 million. After the end of the war, many Korean and Chinese residents, whether out of necessity or desire, continued to reside in Japan. However, because of the strict citizenship requirements, which include blood ties, they have found it difficult to become naturalized citizens. Finally, there are estimated two million *burakumin*—descendants of outcasts—who continue to be discriminated against.[18]

In the 1970s, Honda's concern with U.S. racism led to his investigation of Japanese minorities, Japanese racism, and some of the consequences of Japanese colonialism. He investigated the forced migration of Korean workers to Japan during World War II. He also explored Japanese neocolonial relations with contemporary Southeast Asia, as exemplified by his essay "The 'Export' of Women from the Philippines," which appears in Part II of this book. He is one of the few well-known journalists who has covered the topic of racism in contemporary Japanese society.

The Pursuit of Japanese War Responsibility

Just as Honda's critique of U.S. racism became transmuted into a critique of Japanese racism, his condemnation of U.S. imperialism and what he perceived to be war crimes led him to a closer examination of Japan's past. His political awareness became self-reflective as he launched a long-standing and controversial investigation of Japan's role in the Fifteen Years' War. (The term denotes the fifteen-year period from the invasion of Manchuria in 1931 to the end of the Pacific war in 1945, during which time Japan was continuously engaged in military activity in China.)

Anticipating the 1972 normalization of relations between Japan and the People's Republic of China, in 1971 he traveled to China with the intention of reporting on the war from the Chinese perspective. Just as his reporting on the Vietnam war reflected the viewpoint of the Vietnamese peasants, his interviews and analyses sought to convey the perspective of the victims of Japanese aggression. Honda's self-defined task was to present the logic of the side being killed, rather than the logic of the side doing the killing, as most Japanese reporters had done during and after the war. His interviews resulted in two major books, *Journey to China,* published in 1972 and *The Emperor's Military,* published in 1975.

Honda's foray into the forgotten past of Japanese war atrocities and his pursuit of Japanese war guilt shocked many readers and increasingly put him in conflict with the Japanese right. From the early 1970s on, he was one of their favorite targets, a testament to his ability to cause ire among right-wing politicians and publishers. As long as his critique focused on the United States, he did not threaten any major interest group in Japan, but Japan's sordid military past was another matter. The right-wing attack has been spearheaded by the publishing house Bungei Shunjû and its flagship journal, *Bungei Shunjû.*

In 1937, the invading Japanese army killed hundreds of thousands of Chinese in Nanjing. Although Honda commented on the Nanjing massacre in only one chapter of *Journey to China,* in doing so he opened a debate that was to last for over two decades. *Bungei Shunjû* and other right-wing publications began a concerted attack on his allegations. The right at first attempted to downplay the extent of the massacre and, later, to deny its existence altogether. The conflict escalated during the 1970s and 1980s as the issue provoked historical and journalistic research, in addition to a tremendous amount of polemic.[19]

The debate over the Nanjing massacre occurred in the context of a series of controversies over the content of history textbooks. The most significant struggle was a number of court cases that began in 1965 over a history of Japan by a well-known writer of history, Ienaga Saburô. The Ministry of Education censored the book because it contained passages about Japanese war crimes and atrocities.[20] Another textbook controversy flared up in 1982 when the Ministry of Education approved a history textbook that described the Japanese military's entry into China as an "advance" rather than invasion. This was followed by another round of controversy in 1985.[21]

Honda's criticism extends to the Japanese peace movement. He faults the "peaceniks" for failing to understand Japan's war responsibility, arguing that their ritual invocations of Hiroshima and Nagasaki obfuscate their own prior crime of military aggression. In insisting that World War II was a war of aggression by Japan, Honda stands nearly alone in challenging both the dominant Japanese consensus on the war as a "tragedy" and the general amnesia of Japanese war responsibility.

Why is the question of Japanese war responsibility and war guilt so significant? For Honda, there is, first of all, the problem of ethics. After the Tokyo War Crimes Trial and partly as a result of the U.S. Cold War policy, which rehabilitated militaristic politicians while purging leftist leaders, the issue of Japanese war responsibility was all but forgotten except by a handful of intellectuals. The Fifteen Years' War came to be viewed as a "tragic" period in Japanese history, with the moral conclusion being that "war is bad." Indeed, eight years of total war mobilization exhausted both people and resources. When the war ended with the atomic bombing of Hiroshima and Nagasaki, the Japanese people saw themselves collectively as victims rather than as aggressors.[22] But Honda stressed repeatedly that Japanese citizens nevertheless have the obligation to recognize the history of *Japanese* war atrocities and crimes. The amnesia about guilt constitutes a "second crime" (see "The Burden of Being Japanese," in Part I).

Second, the issue of Japanese war responsibility is intimately intertwined with contemporary Japanese politics. Honda is troubled by the Japanese people's acquiescence in allowing war criminals to move into positions of political leadership. He is also critical of the insensitive and militarist actions perpetrated by LDP politicians. In the face of efforts to deny the Nanjing massacre, to revive remnants of prewar militarism, and to resuscitate the Japanese military, the issue of war responsibility plays a central role in Japanese politics.

Critique of Corruption and Complacency

In the 1970s, Honda began to chronicle the corruption and complacency of Japanese political life. While his criticisms have tended to focus on individual leaders, he points out that these personal scandals are merely symptoms of the deeper failure of the postwar political system. The separation of executive, judicial, and legislative branches has vanished under LDP dominance. Simultaneously, the machinations of LDP politicians inevitably revolve around financial considerations. Corruption and scandal are structural features of the Japanese political scene.

In the 1980s, peace and prosperity continued to generate popular support for the Liberal Democratic Party. Prime Minister Nakasone Yasuhiro played a role in Japan similar to that of Ronald Reagan in the United States and Margaret Thatcher in Great Britain. Like his counterparts, Nakasone combined a conservative domestic economic and social policy with an activist foreign policy. For example, he privatized publicly owned industries, most significantly the Japan National Railways, while increasing the defense budget so that by 1987 it exceeded the traditional limit of 1 percent of GNP. Perhaps most symbolic was his controversial public "worship" at Yasukuni Shrine on August 15, 1985, the fortieth anniversary of the end of World War II. Yasukuni Shrine commemorates dead war heroes, including many who were deemed war criminals during World War II. This public commemoration raised the specter of prewar Japanese militarism and imperialism and provoked criticism not only within Japan but from neighboring Asian countries as well.[23]

Simultaneously, Nakasone articulated a vision of an "internationalized" Japan—an economically powerful Japan that was to play a major role in international affairs. His active involvement in international affairs was a major departure from the customary behavior of past prime ministers, who had largely relied on the Foreign Ministry for the conception and execution of foreign policy. In particular, he sought to forge close personal ties with the United States and Ronald Reagan; this resulted in the friendship that was celebrated by the Japanese mass media as the "Ron-Yasu" relationship.

The 1980s witnessed a series of scandals that were never completely resolved. Nakasone's successor, Takeshita Noboru, ran into serious domestic challenges, most notably from the Recruit scandal. The Recruit Company, a job placement agency, had been illegally selling stocks to leading politicians in the LDP and other parties. Furthermore, one of Nakasone's legislative efforts, the imposition of a 3 percent consumption tax, fueled voter dissatisfaction with the party. In 1988, the loss of popular support forced the resignation of Takeshita and his cabinet, including Minister of Finance

Miyazawa Kiichi. Because the scandal involved virtually the entire leadership of the LDP, the search for Takeshita's successor focused on finding a noncontroversial candidate. Uno Yôsuke, a relatively unknown LDP politician, was tapped to be the successor. However, almost immediately after assuming power, he became mired in a major scandal involving an alleged dalliance with a call girl.

In spite of efforts to defuse the problem and defend Uno—analyzed by Honda in "Is Prostitution a Women's Problem?" which appears in Part V of this volume—the scandal and the weakening support exhibited in the 1989 Upper House election led to Uno's disgrace and resignation. After a furious intranecine struggle among the LDP leadership, Kaifu Toshiki, an obscure LDP Diet member, succeeded Uno. Yet in 1991, in the next contest to determine the LDP leader, and hence the Japanese prime minister, Miyazawa emerged triumphant. The man who had been forced to resign only three years before came back to take the leadership of the LDP and hence of Japan.

An outside observer might well ask an obvious question: Why do Japanese voters continue to support the corrupt and scandal-ridden LDP politicians and regimes? Honda suggests a number of reasons, including the collusion of the bureaucracy and the media and the overwhelming reliance on money in Japanese politics. His most sustained discussion of this issue emerged in the mid-1970s. The disclosure of Prime Minister Tanaka Kakuei's involvement in the Lockheed scandal, which involved a military contractor's bribery of top LDP politicians, was expected to lead to his defeat. However, the people of his district re-elected him by an overwhelming margin. Honda's investigation led him to conclude that in spite of Tanaka's corruption, voters felt that he understood their problems and sufferings. As he wrote:

> Since the Meiji period, Tokyo regimes have continued to rule the countryside—the periphery, the place without the sun, the victims of the postwar high-speed growth. The anger, pain, and resentment of the side being trampled upon against urban, smart, elite people of the side where the sun shines underlies the 17,000 votes for Tanaka.[24]

Honda's political sociology differs from those who blamed the stupidity and ignorance of the people who voted for Tanaka. Rather, he attempted to comprehend the psychology and logic of the exploited farmers who vented their anger on the center and the privileged. That their resistance results in the victory of one of the men who was responsible for the underdevelopment of the countryside does not negate the failures of postwar economic policy or the shortcomings of the elite.

The Impoverished Intellectuals

As I have noted, the intellectual discourse of the immediate postwar years was dominated by progressives. Whether opposing the renewal of the security treaty between Japan and the United States or criticizing U.S. intervention in Vietnam, the dominant tenor was decidedly anti-LDP. Yet no group has been on the receiving end of Honda's ire, sarcasm, and polemic more than the "impoverished" intellectuals of this period. He is relentlessly critical of the hypocrisy and complacency that he feels is rife among cultural leaders. His debates and criticisms have been a direct challenge to the left establishment and its increasing rightward drift through the 1970s and 1980s.

With the growth of the Japanese economy and the mounting contradictions in Eastern Europe and the Soviet Union, an increasing number of Japanese intellectuals withdrew from the progressive camp and began to ally themselves with the forces willing to sustain the status quo. A trickle in the early 1970s had turned into a flood by the late 1980s. In the heyday of the Nakasone regime in the 1980s, it became commonplace for intellectuals to announce that they were ready to renounce their leftist past and squarely face the reality at hand.[25]

Honda's concern over this rightward drift stemmed in part from a historical parallel to the prewar period, when intellectuals—many of them former Communists—renounced their leftist past and converted (*tenkô*) to the nationalistic and militarist ideology that led to the catastrophe of the Fifteen Years' War.[26] The amnesia about Japanese war responsibility was therefore linked to a possible resurgence of militarism and authoritarianism.

Honda's explanation of corruption included a critique of the money and prestige associated with the major establishment publishers. For example, a large publishing house like Bungei Shunjû allocates money and prestige to promising young writers who are willing to work within its ideological framework. The constraints that major publishing houses place on their writers thus create the condition for corrupting intellectuals.

However, as with his analysis of Japanese politics, Honda's critique of intellectuals is ultimately ethical and personal. For example, he has been extremely critical of the postwar progressive novelist Oe Kenzaburô. Although widely regarded as an embodiment of the left establishment, Oe collaborates with the publishing house Bungei Shunjû, which is the preeminent conservative publisher, sponsoring works that deny the Nanjing massacre and promote reactionary causes. Honda emphasizes the contradiction and hypocrisy of espousing progressive ideals while simultaneously working with a reactionary publisher. Indeed, a heated exchange between Honda and Oe enlivened the pages of *Asahi Jânaru* in the mid-1980s.

Critical of the political establishment throughout his journalistic career, Honda's growing disenchantment with the left establishment, which had lionized him in the late 1960s, is noticeable by the 1980s. For Honda, the rightward drift of the cultural and intellectual elite from the 1970s represents an ethical and political failure. It is another manifestation of the corruption and spiritual impoverishment of postwar Japanese society.

Conformity in a Tadpole Society

Honda characterizes Japan as a "tadpole society." Tadpoles, he observes, swim in schools, without leaders or mutual consent; a random movement by one member leads others to imitate it blindly. He argues that Japanese social life has become increasingly devoid of individual and critical thinking, logic, and ethics. Their absence in the tadpole society explains, at least in part, the country's failure to come to terms with its war responsibility as well as its corrupt and complacent political and intellectual life.

The fundamental cause of the tadpole society is the Ministry of Education, which dictates "standardized" education that stresses memorization and regurgitation above all other intellectual faculties. Rather than fostering creativity or individual development, the bureaucracy stifles imagination and self-expression. In the end, the Ministry of Education's policy simply reproduces this narrow and rigid bureaucratic thinking among Japanese youth.

In the late 1970s, Honda investigated the growing social concern over the "problem" of children, which was published in 1979 as *The Revenge of Children*. Many dysfunctions he observed in disturbed children, such as violence, stemmed from the overly rigid and bureaucratic schooling to which they were subject. As he concludes in "Standardized Education" (Part III): "The 'problem' with children is in fact the 'problem' with society." The excessive pressure to excel in college entrance examinations, which are the key to elite schools and hence to elite jobs, creates narrow and selfish children, who then go on to work in places like the Ministry of Education.[27] The reproduction of bureaucratic thinking and social structure ultimately underlies the failure of Japanese educational policy.

Thus, it is not surprising that the Ministry of Education contributes to the amnesia of war responsibility, as, for example, by its direct censorship of textbooks. However, even more damaging is its ability to extinguish the critical spirit and individual thinking of Japanese children.

Another manifestation of the tadpole society is Japan's cultural conformity and dependence. Because of its dominant influence after World War II, the United States became the ideal that Japanese society strove to emulate. The insistent need to internationalize Japan has a progressive aspect insofar as it reflects the desire to cast away a "tradition" associated with fascism and militarism. But another aspect of the desire to modernize Japan is a colonial mentality, which perceives the United States and Europe as culturally superior. Hence, Japanese society is awash with English-language signs and publications, Western models and designs. These manifestations of Western cultural imperialism find their domestic roots in the tadpole mentality, which is devoid of any deep conviction or sustaining principles.

A casual visitor to Japan is often surprised by the ubiquity of English-language signs, Western female models, and other evidence of Western culture. As many young Americans found out in the 1980s, there are numerous well-paid English-language teaching jobs in Japan. Honda and other critics argue that the canonization of English as *the* foreign language is not only ethnocentric but a symptom of the enormous influence of the United States in Japanese life. Indeed, some intellectuals argue that the Japanese language is inherently illogical—a species of Japanese exceptionalism that conveys a colonial intellectual mentality.

Many traditional Japanese practices have been superseded by the Western, or American, ideal. In effect, the Westernization of Japanese clothing, mores, and arts symbolizes a form of cultural dependency and, ultimately, a failure of the independent Japanese spirit. Honda's essay "Why Can't We Squat?" (Part III) is a polemic against the Westernization of Japanese attire and posture. In finding that the men from his hometown looked "strange" in Western suits, Honda's essay recalls John Berger's essay on "The Suit and the Photograph": "The suit, as we know it today, developed in Europe as a professional ruling-class costume in the last third of the nineteenth century. Almost anonymous as a uniform, it was the first ruling-class costume to idealize purely *sedentary power*."[28] Berger notes that peasants who wear them look "physically mis-shapen"; they seem "coarse, clumsy, brutelike. And incorrigibly so." Honda argues that traditional Japanese attire and customs are functional; he is against mock "internationalization" that blindly denounces everything Japanese and advocates everything Western.

The Environmental Crisis as a Political Problem

Honda's enchantment with mountains dates from his highschool years but his coverage of Vietnam was critical to his analysis of the environmental crisis as a *political* problem. His mountaineering interests, as well as his early fascination with the world of insects, instilled a lasting interest in and reverence for the natural world and a concern for the rapidly declining environment. However, rather than the depoliticized understanding of the degradation of the environment common among ecologists, his writings after 1970 offer distinctly political analyses. In particular, he is critical of the two chief agents of environmental destruction, corporations and the state.

Honda's environmental writings are also some of the most personal of his essays. Part of the power of his essays stem from the personal dimension he brings to his concerns. The extensive use of pesticides and pollution had, by the 1960s, wreaked considerable damage on the Japanese archipelago. In "Disfigured Tadpoles" (Part IV), he writes eloquently of the vanished world of his childhood. It is his hometown that is being destroyed. Honda's nostalgic invocation brings together the death of his parents and the demise of the natural world of his youth.

The proliferation of pollution-related diseases, exemplified by Minamata (a disease caused by mercury poisoning), became a topic of great interest in the late 1960s. Honda does not cover these pollution-related diseases directly, however. He writes by combining the personal and the political, bemoaning the loss of the diverse and lively world of his childhood on the one hand, while castigating environmental degradation and invasion in the name of development on the other.

In the 1960s, Tanaka Kakuei, the future prime minister, gained popular attention by calling for "the renovation of the Japanese archipelago" (*Nihon rettô kaizô*). His call represented the *bêtes noires* of the environment—real estate and tourist capital. Industrialization and urbanization led inevitably to the transformation of the countryside, as farming villages were replaced by industrial centers and tourist resorts.

The destruction of the physical environment is ultimately caused by political and economic factors. Once again, *mondai ishiki*—"problem consciousness"—provides a critical perspective on a deleterious trend in Japanese life. Honda is steadfast in blaming the "developmentalist" and environmentally destructive policies of the LDP and the bureaucracies, as well as the selfish interests of tourist and real estate capital. Simultaneously, however, he stresses the human costs of environmental destruction. For example, the development of Hokkaido is problematic not simply because of the environmental destruction but because of the costs to the native Ainu people's way of life. In defending the way of life of dispossessed minorities and increasingly marginalized people dependent on farming and fishing, he condemns the logic of "invasion."

Further, he is deeply sympathetic to the seemingly "reactionary" opinion of other victims, such as farmers:

> For those who have been hurt for generations by nature, the propensity to regard modern civilization as the source of evil or the desire to return to the "primitive" or protect nature against "development" seem like the leisurely plaything of urbanites. At least, they have been forced to hold this view.[30]

In short, he not only advocates the environmental cause for its intrinsic merit, but argues vociferously on the side of the victims.

Journalism as a Calling

Throughout his career, Honda has taken enormous pride in his craft. He has written extensively on the skills involved in journalism, ranging from methods of reporting to techniques of writing. And he has argued passionately for the crucial importance of moral commitment to the enterprise of journalism.

The Technique of Japanese Composition was published in 1976. Originally presented as a series of public lectures, it became a bestseller. And although Honda bemoans the lack of interest in the craft of composition, this book has been a critical resource for many students and aspiring writers. Above all, Honda stresses clarity of expression: he criticizes obfuscation, which hides a lack of logic or thought.

Honda's journalistic method is to listen to the people who are affected by the events he covers. Here his method approaches that of anthropological fieldwork, in which the investigator spends time living and talking with people.

Honda argues that journalistic objectivity necessarily entails reporting different points of view. But where others have written from the winner's or aggressor's perspective, he redresses the balance and contributes to the debate by compiling and presenting the loser's or victim's point of view. For example, when he was roundly criticized for his "one-sided" reporting of Japanese military atrocities in China, he responded:

> Every day, everything, completely, without omission, without exception, Japan has been reporting for many decades since the Sino-Japanese War on China only from the perspective of Japan (more accurately, the perspective of Japanese leaders).[31]

Honda is well known for calling himself a "newspaper journalist." In Japan, where corporate identification is strong, it is striking that he does not actively seek to identify himself with his prestigious employer, *Asahi Shinbun*. This is a manifestation of his independent spirit, but also of his deep identification with the calling of journalism as a lifelong vocation. It is his ethical and professional commitment that allows him to break taboos and write critical pieces—increasingly a rarity in Japanese intellectual life.

Conclusion

In 1992, Honda retired from *Asahi Shinbun*. In the same year, *Asahi Jânaru*, Japan's leading progressive weekly which had published many of Honda's pieces, folded. These two events marked the end of an era in postwar Japanese history.

Nonetheless, Honda has not settled into a sedentary life. In "A Manifesto for Independent Journalism," the last essay in this volume, he decries the corruption of mainstream journalism, which is beholden to corporate interests and the powers that be. He then outlines his plan for a new progressive daily, which will be independent and pursue true journalism. True journalism entails respect for the facts, concern for the oppressed, and independence of judgment.

In addition to this major project, Honda continues to write a weekly column for *Sunday Mainichi* under the heading "The Impoverished Spirit." He addresses the same themes he has been developing since the late 1960s: corruption, war responsibility, latent and manifest racism and neocolonialism, cowardly and complacent intellectuals, ecological disasters, cultural dependency and false "internationalization," and the general spiritual impoverishment of Japanese political and intellectual life. At the same time, he has plans to go on mountaineering expeditions, return to school to pursue various topics of interest, and travel far and wide.

Honda's enormous popularity and influence derives in part from his central role in post-Vietnam war Japanese political and intellectual circles. Lionized by the left establishment, he has remained on center stage in the major postwar debates. It is only partly ironic that his ethical and personal critique of the "tadpole society" should find so many eager readers in Japan today. Perhaps it is a reason to hope that Japan will not retrace its steps on the road that Honda inveighs against—the prewar road of militarism, authoritarianism, and imperialism.

Because of his courage, independence, and commitment to truth and justice, Honda remains a paragon of critical journalism. He has been a formidable force against the impoverished spirit in contemporary Japanese political and intellectual life.

A Note on the Translation

Honda's essays have been translated by Eri Fujieda, Masayuki Hamazaki, and myself. In no way is the English version a faithful and literal rendition of the Japanese original. Many passages have been deleted or shifted, while others have been augmented. In Japan, Honda is widely regarded as a master stylist; our version cannot quite aspire to that level, and often lacks the verve of Honda's direct and aggressive prose. But we have attempted to render Honda's essays comprehensible to English-speaking (particularly North American) readers, and we have altered the original text only to make Honda's arguments and ideas more accessible. The substance of his message remains unaltered, and Honda has made time in his busy schedule to facilitate and approve the translation.

Nonetheless, Honda's prose loses something in translation. Perhaps it is in the nature of journalistic writings that they don't survive cultural transfer very well. Journalistic writings stress contemporaneity, and are prone to ephemerality even within that culture. It is not surprising that what is of interest to a particular group of people at a particular time may be of only passing interest to other groups at other times. Yet it is also true that by their very particularity and ephemerality, Honda's essays are the best testament of that particular place and time.

Honda's own notes have been incorporated into the text as much as possible. All explanatory footnotes are by the editor. Some offer background information, while others give bibliographic references. When Honda cites passages from foreign authors or speakers, we have rendered them from the Japanese-language text. East Asian authors are listed surname first, unless they write in English, as for example Mr. Hamazaki and Ms. Fujieda. Because using the Japanese titles of Honda's works and providing English translations in each case would be cumbersome, I have used my own English translations of titles in the text. An abbreviated chronology of his writings is included below.

A final note. Honda has very definite ideas of his own (expounded at length in various places) about the craft of writing and, in particular, the Romanization of Japanese words. However, for the benefit of English-language readers, we have used the McCune-Reischauer system (close to the Hepburn, or the Hebon, system widely used in Japan) to transliterate Japanese words into the Roman alphabet. Interested readers may refer to *The Impoverished Spirit*, vol. 9.

I wish to thank John Bellamy Foster and Susan Lowes for their enthusiasm, the *sine qua non* of this project, Martha Cameron for copy editing, and Beth Stroud. Thanks also to Nancy Abelmann for her support.

I have dedicated this book to my friends at the Kawasaki Peace Information Centre, and especially to Uemura Hideaki and Tenmyô Ako. Uemura introduced me to Honda's *The Technique of Japanese Composition* when I was struggling to write several essays in Japanese seven years ago. I would also like to thank my friends in Japan for their support, including Moriya Fumiaki, Makamura Keiko, Watanabe Hideki, and Alan Wolfe.

I have long admired Honda's courageous journalism and trenchant criticism; it is my pleasure to introduce him to the Anglophone public.

John Lie

Notes

1. The survey was conducted by the University Cooperative Association. Natsume Sôseki, perhaps Japan's most influential novelist, was number two, followed by popular contemporary novelists Shima Ryôtarô, Akagawa Jirô, and Murakami Haruki. To be sure, Honda fared worse in other categories. For example, Honda's titles ranked eighteenth among the "most moving books" that students have read. Natsume was first in this category.

2. See Michael Schaller, *The American Occupation of Japan* (New York: Oxford University Press, 1985).

3. In the course of the Tokyo War Crimes Trial, war criminals were separated into three classes, with Class A being the most serious. Seven Class A war criminals—most significantly, Tôjô Hideki—were executed. See R.H. Minear, *Victors' Justice: The Tokyo War Crimes Trial* (Princeton: Princeton University Press, 1971).

4. See Karel van Wolferen, *The Enigma of Japanese Power* (New York: Knopf, 1989); and Nathaniel B. Thayer, *How the Conservatives Rule Japan* (Princeton: Princeton University Press, 1969).

5. See, for example, J. A. A. Stockwin, *Japan: Divided Politics in a Growth Economy,* 2nd ed. (New York: W. W. Norton, 1982).

6. Shinshû is the old name for what is today Nagano Prefecture. The area is mountainous and well known for its sericulture. Honda claims that people of Shinshû are known for being logical and argumentative.

7. Okazaki Yôzô suggests that Honda likes to do what others have not done. Hence, once Mount Everest was "conquered," Honda lost his initial enthusiasm. See Okazaki, *Honda Katsuichi no kenkyû* [A study of Honda Katsuichi] (Tokyo: Banseisha, 1990), pp. 39–42.

8. In a well-known critique of Honda, Hino Keizô, a novelist, praises Honda's early works largely because of their lack of political and social content. See Hino, "Honda Katsuichi: shuzaisarerugawa ni tatsu hôdôsha" ["Honda Katsuichi: The reporter who is reported upon"], *Chûô Kôron,* May 1973.

9. Honda, "Fâburu konchûki" ["Fabre's *Entomological Souvenirs*"], *Sekai,* May 1985.

10. Marilyn B. Young, *The Vietnam Wars, 1945-1990* (New York: HarperCollins, 1991), p. 175.

11. Many Japanese journalists died in Vietnam while they covered the war. Honda is critical of U.S. journalists, whom he compares to prewar Japanese journalists who merely reported what the government said. He also salutes his wartime friends who died in the course of covering the war. See Honda's "Betonamu de shinda 'senyû' tachi no daiben" ["Speaking up for wartime friends in Vietnam"], in *Jijitsu to wa nanika* (Tokyo: Asahi Shinbunsha, 1975/1984).

12. See Thomas R.H. Havens, *Fire Across the Sea* (Princeton: Princeton University Press, 1987), pp. 35–53.

13. It was later published in English as *Vietnam War* by Miraisha in 1972. On Beheiren and its effort to send Honda's book abroad, see Ishida Takeshi, *Nihon no seiji to kotoba* [Politics and words in Japan], vol. 2 (Tokyo: Tokyo Daigaku Shuppankai, 1989), pp. 116–120.

14. "Maiami rengô kara Betonamu made no Gasshûkoku no michinori" ["The path of the United States from the Miami League to Vietnam"], in *Korosareru gawa no ronri* (Tokyo: Asahi Shinbunsha, 1982), pp. 27–28.

15. "Tanken sarerugawa no ronri" ["The logic of the explored"], in *Korosareru gawa no ronri*, p. 214. See also "Hôdô to bunka jinruigaku o megutte" ["Concerning reporting and cultural anthropology"] in *Jijitsu to wa nanika*.

16. See, for example, M. I. Hilger, *Together with the Ainu* (Norman: University of Oklahoma Press, 1971).

17. Honda, "Shakudatsusha Shamo ni torubeki michi wa aruka" ["Is there a path for the exploiter Japanese?"], *Korosarerugawa no ronri*, p. 248.

18. See, for example, Ian Neary, *Political Protest and Social Control in Pre-war Japan* (Atlantic Highlands: Humanities Press, 1989) on the burakumin; Michael Weiner, *The Origins of the Korean Community in Japan, 1910–1923* (Atlantic Highlands: Humanities Press, 1989) and John Lie, "The Discriminated Fingers," *Monthly Review* 38 (1987) on the Koreans.

19. See especially Honda's *Nankin e no michi* [The road to Nanjing] (Tokyo: Asahi Shinbunsha, 1989).

20. See R. P. Dore, "Textbook Censorship in Japan: The Ienaga Case," *Pacific Affairs* 43 (1970-71); and Saburô Ienaga, "The Historical Significance of the Japanese Textbook Lawsuit," *Bulletin of Concerned Asian Scholars* 2 (1970).

21. See, for example, Chong-sik Lee, "History and Politics in Japanese-Korean Relations: The Textbook Controversy and Beyond," *Journal of Northeast Asian Studies* 2 (1983).

22. On wartime Japan, see Thomas R. H. Havens, *Valley of Darkness* (New York: W. W. Norton, 1978). On the topic of war responsibility, see Ienaga Saburô, *Sensô sekinin* [War responsibility] (Tokyo: Iwanami Shoten, 1985); and John Lie, "War, Absolution, and Amnesia: The Decline of War Responsibility in Postwar Japan," *Peace and Change* 16 (1991).

23. Helen Hardacre, *Shinto and the State, 1868–1988* (Princeton: Princeton University Press, 1989), especially pp. 150–53. See also Norma Fields, *In the Realm of the Dying Emperor* (New York: Pantheon, 1991).

24. Honda Katsuichi, "Tanaka Kakuei o asshôsaseta gawa no shinri to ronri" ["The psychology and logic of the side that gave Tanaka Kakuei a resounding victory"] in *Soshite waga sokoku, Nippon* (Tokyo: Asahi Shinbunsha, 1983), p. 230.

25. See John Lie, "Reactionary Marxism," *Monthly Review* 38 (1987).

26. On *tenkô*, see Kazuko Tsurumi, *Social Change and the Individual* (Princeton: Princeton University Press, 1970).

27. See Thomas Rohlen, *Japan's High Schools* (Berkeley: University of California Press, 1983); and John Lie, "Japanese Education as Number One," *Bulletin of Concerned Asian Scholars* 21 (1989).

28. John Berger, *About Looking* (New York: Pantheon, 1980), p. 34

29. Ibid., p. 31

30. Honda, "Tanaka Kakuei," p. 227. I am reminded of John Berger's moving "Historical Afterword" in his *Pig Earth* (New York: Pantheon, 1979).

31. Honda, "'Ippôteki na hôdô' to iu ippôteki hinan" ["One-sided criticism of 'One-sided Reporting'"] in *Jijitsu to wa nanika*, p. 64.

Chronology
and Chief Publications

1932 Honda Katsuichi is born in Nagano Prefecture (formerly Shinshû).
1950 Enrolls in Chiba University and studies pharmacy.
1954 Graduates from Chiba University; enrolls in Kyoto University and studies genetics.
1958 Publishes his first book, *The Unknown Himalaya*, based on his trip the year before; starts working for *Asahi Shinbun*.
1963 Lives with the Inuit of northern Canada; publishes *Canada, Eskimo*.
1964 Lives with the natives of New Guinea, publishes *New Guinea Highlanders*.
1965 Lives with the Bedouins; writes *Arabian Pastoral People* (published in 1966).
1966 Goes to South Vietnam.
1968 Publishes *The Villages of War*, which becomes a bestseller.
1969 Lives in Harlem, New York; writes *The United States of America* (1970).

1971   Goes to China and Albania; writes *Journey to China* (1972).

1972   *Vietnam: A Voice from the Villages* is released.

1974   The first volume of *Hinkon naru seishin* [The impoverished spirit] is published.

1975   Returns to South Vietnam after the fall of Saigon.

1978   Goes to Cambodia; publishes *What Is Happening to Cambodia?*

1980   Returns to Cambodia to report on the Pol Pot massacre; writes *Journey to Cambodia* (published in 1981); tenth volume of *The Impoverished Spirit* appears.

1983   Goes to China to investigate the Nanjing massacre.

1987   *The Road to Nanjing* is published; begins to retrace the journey of Magellan.

1988   The twentieth volume of *The Impoverished Spirit* appears.

1989   *Magellan Came!* is published; Honda reports on Australian aborigines.

1990   Travels to East Germany; *The German Democratic Republic* is released.

1992   Retires from *Asahi Shinbun*; begins planning for a new daily.

I
Against Amnesia and Complacency: Japanese War Responsibility

The Fifteen Years' War
as a War of Invasion

What did Japan do to China between 1931 and 1945? In a word, invade. However, the mass media never use this word, referring instead to the Fifteen Years' War.[*] Is there a difference between war and invasion? I think so.

Let me offer an analogy. If you do not resist a thief—let him steal and do as he will—there will be no fight. Or, if a woman gives in to a rapist without overt resistance, then there will be no conflict. If she should resist, however, there will be a struggle. An invasion is like theft or rape. If there is no resistance, then there will be no war. War is like ordinary fighting. Thus to say that war is bad is like saying "Fighting is bad." As long as one is willing to suffer, there will be no fighting, no war. If one deems fighting to be bad, both parties will be punished. Or one could say that the one who was stolen

---

[*] Many historians date the Japanese involvement in World War II from the time of the Manchurian incident in 1931—hence the Fifteen Years' War.

from is just as bad as the one who attempted to steal—after all, that is how the fighting began. Such a statement distorts the reality of the problem; I say that the same holds true for war.

There are of course wars without invasion. However, there can be no doubt that the Fifteen Years' War, at least in regard to China, occurred because Japan invaded China. After December 1941, Japan waged a war against Europe and the United States—the so-called Pacific war. It is possible to say that this was a war between invaders. However, the war with China was an invasion. For the mass media to call it a war is to hide the truth.

Most Japanese have trouble understanding the meaning of the word "invasion." This is partly because Japan has suffered relatively few invasions. Except for Okinawa, which became a battleground at the end of the Pacific war, most areas have not experienced an invasion. Therefore, for the Japanese, invasion is always something that happens to others. They may read books about it or see it in movies, but they do not know it firsthand. Even in the case of movies, there are very few that deal with the reality of the Japanese invasion. The Japanese war in China is the subject of *Shinkû chitai* (The Vacuum Zone).[*] Although it is in many ways an antiwar film, it depicts the internal contradictions of the Japanese army. I know of no major film that makes the *invaded people* the protagonists. This also contributes to the Japanese ignorance of invasion.

---

[*] The film was based on a novel by Noma Hiroshi which became a critical success for its dramatic evocation of the Japanese military and its moral collapse.

Colonialism and Neocolonialism

To be sure, invasion is not unique to Japan. A classic example of European invasion is the expansion of Portugal and Spain. Several years ago, I investigated what happened in Brazil, Argentina, Guam, and elsewhere, which was published as *Magellan Came!* I traced Magellan's journey around the globe to find out how people suffered as a result. The same thing happened in North America to its native inhabitants, as I wrote in *The United States of America.*

What does invasion mean in terms of society and economy? Roughly, colonialism and neocolonialism. The older way is to send the military into the colonized area. Usually, the colonizer takes over the land, kills its native inhabitants, and sends in people from the colonizing country to occupy the land. The original inhabitants of the colonized country who do not die become slaves.

The new type of colonialism occurred after World War II. One might call it indirect invasion, or economic exploitation—it is still tantamount to enslavement.

What Is an Invasion?

The case of the Fifteen Years' War is an instance of classical colonial invasion. What is an invasion? There are five main components. First, murder. Second, pillage, arson, destruction, and other types of physical violence. Third, rape. Fourth, enslavement. Fifth, economic exploitation.

Let's take a closer look at these components.

Murder

The so-called China incident occurred in 1937 and the Nanjing massacre began later that year and lasted into the early part of the following year. Many people believe that the Nanjing massacre occurred in Nanjing, where citizens and prisoners were killed. The reality is a bit different. The battle for Nanjing lasted over forty days, and the Japanese army committed atrocities as it advanced. It is not the case of an orderly army suddenly going berserk once they got to Nanjing. The massacre began the moment they landed in China. It is not possible to draw a clear boundary of the site of the Nanjing massacre, which lasted close to three months.

What did the Japanese soldiers do? On November 22, 1937, about one hundred soldiers entered a hamlet of twelve households and forty-nine people. The residents attempted to escape, but thirty-eight were caught and surrounded. There were two young women: one, a seventeen-year-old; the other, a pregnant woman. The two were separated from the other prisoners, and many Japanese soldiers raped them. The women who were raped were dragged to the garden as other soldiers were setting houses on fire. Soldiers thrust a bamboo stick in the seventeen-year-old's vagina; she died as swords pierced her. The pregnant woman was also disemboweled as soldiers gouged the embryo from her body. Three Chinese men went into a burning house. When they entered the house, Japanese soldiers shut the door as the roof fell on them. A two-year-old boy started to cry. A soldier took the boy away from his mother and threw him into the fire. The mother was pushed into the aqueduct at swordpoint. Thirty-one other people were also pushed into the aqueduct after they were slashed by churning swords. One man who attempted to fight back was cut thirteen times.

How do I know all this? Miraculously, one man survived who witnessed the whole affair.

The Japanese army continued its atrocities as it approached Nanjing. There were many murders—some few in number, some in the hundreds, and some in the thousands. The largest atrocity involved over 14,000 people, according to a newspaper report from that time.

One Japanese soldier, Tanaka, was involved in killing prisoners and later recounted the horror to me. Japanese soldiers surrounded prisoners and took them to a river. Soldiers stood in a semicircle and showered bullets on the gathered prisoners. It was a scene from hell.

Tanaka can never forget the gigantic human columns built by prisoners who sought to escape the bullets. He does not understand quite how these human columns were created, but they came into being as people who could not escape to the sides or into the ground attempted to evade the bullets by stepping over dead bodies. These human columns collapsed three times. In order to prevent negative international coverage and condemnation, no prisoner was allowed to survive to recount the horror.

Tanaka's division spent all night processing the dead bodies. It was nearly impossible to get rid of all of them—there were over 10,000. One method was to burn them. Because people were wearing thick cotton winter clothes, they burned easily. Once bodies began to burn, it became bright and easier to work. Furthermore, prisoners could no longer feign death. Some who seemed dead began to move—they were shot immediately. The cleaning up went on and on. After the soldiers had taken care of a mountain of dead bodies, a new division came to help. At this point, gasoline was poured on the dead bodies and they were burnt. The corpses couldn't be washed down the river because most of them retained their human form; it was important to change the form as much as possible. However, there wasn't enough gasoline, and so a mountain of blackened corpses remained. About 13,500 people were ultimately killed.

After this story was reported in *Mainichi Shinbun*, Japanese right-wing and far-right groups began to harass the man who testified. After repeated harassment, the man ultimately lowered the number from 13,500 to 4,000 or 5,000.

These examples are all taken from the early period of the Japanese invasion of China. Eventually, Chiang Kai-shek's army retreated but the People's Liberation Army under Mao Zedong became more active. The Japanese army often exterminated an entire village that was cooperating with the guerrillas. For example, a village of 1,300 people was attacked by the army in 1940. The army surrounded the village, threw people into burning houses, and shot them. As a result, 1,230 out of 1,300 were killed. To be sure, this is not on the same scale as the Nanjing massacre, but it indicates a policy of annihilation continued throughout the war.

Pillage

Next, robbery, arson, and destruction. Let me offer simple examples.

First, robbery. The following is an excerpt from the wartime diary of a division leader, Nakajima:

> We are inside Nanjing.... Even though I placed a placard saying "Division Leader's Office," people have messed up the whole room and taken from it whatever was noteworthy, even junk. I collected all the remainder and put it in a closet and closed it, but to no avail. The day after, whatever was there had all been taken away.

In effect, this officer is angry because what he hoped to plunder was plundered by other soldiers.

As an example of arson, the following testimony comes from an information officer:

> In heavy rain, soldiers would run into nearby farmhouses for ten- or fifteen-minute rests. After throwing the farmers out, they gathered chairs and other pieces of furniture and burned them. The clothes that were dripping wet dried quickly by the bonfire.... Thus, a short rest would lead to the burning of farmers' furniture. What for poor farmers were important and treasured objects became logs for Japanese soldiers.

For Chinese peasants, furniture like tables and chairs were very important, far more important than cars are to Japanese people today. However, Japanese soldiers would burn them in order to dry their wet clothes.

Rape

There are so many instances of rape, but let me offer just one example. The woman I interviewed was fifty-seven, which means she must have been seven at the time of the Nanjing massacre. She lived in Nanjing in a family of nine. Many people left Nanjing when they heard about the encroaching Japanese army, but her family and a neighboring family remained:

Suddenly, there was a loud knock on the door. The neighbor and my father went to open the door. As soon as they opened the door, they were shot to death. Surprised, four of us went into the bed and covered ourselves with a blanket. Eventually many people seemed to enter the house. Because I was covered with the blanket, I could not see but I could hear the steps. Simultaneously, there was a gun-shot—my grandfather was shot. Right afterward, the blanket was taken away. There were many soldiers standing there. My grandmother came to protect us; she was immediately shot. I could see the white brain spurting out of my grandmother's head. I fainted so I didn't see what happened afterward. After some time, I regained consciousness as my four-year-old sister was crying. It was still bright outside. She was crying under a blanket.... On the same bed, one of my sisters (thirteen years old at the time) lay dead. Her lower parts were naked and both legs were thrown on the floor. In front of the bed was the corpse of my grandmother. Near the door was my grandfather's corpse. And my older sister (fifteen at the time) was in another bed, dead—the lower part of her body was naked and both legs were thrown on the floor.

Enslavement

There are, roughly, two types of enslavement. One is domestic enslavement; the other is enforced migration to Japan in order to work in coal mines or construction.

There were many types of internal forced labor. The people were often simply rounded up. More generally, the Japanese military asked each village to supply several men. Because landlords still controlled villages, they would force some villagers to comply with the request. They were often taken to coal mines in Manchuria. There were also many who were enslaved abroad. They were forcefully taken to coal mines in Kyushu or Hokkaido or to work in various construction sites.

In Hokkaido, there was a man who escaped and kept on hiding for thirteen years after the end of the war.

Let me cite one testimony from Hokkaido:

> Chinese farmers were forcefully gathered on a piece of land. As needed, they would be used in various chores. Sometimes they would become tenants. The "developing" area in Hokkaido was nothing but the enslavement of farmers.

Economic Exploitation

In reality, this is the most important result of the invasion. After the initial stage of war, large corporations begin to advance. They exploit enforced labor and the low-wage workforce as the colonial economy comes into being.

What Is Characteristic About Japan?

The reality of the Japanese invasion was horrifying. However, invasion is not unique to Japan. The fundamental difference between Japan and others is the ways in which the Japanese take responsibility for the atrocities.

Recently, another writer criticized me: "We are bothered by people like Honda, who claims to represent the Japanese people and apologizes to China for war crimes." However, I never apologized when I was doing research in China. In fact, I have been doing the opposite: I don't apologize, and I say that I don't need to apologize.

What I mean is that when the Nanjing massacre occurred, I was just a child. As a young child, I have no direct responsibility for war crimes. Therefore, even though the war was a Japanese crime, I have no intention of apologizing to the Chinese people. The problem is not in the past, but rather in the present. Twenty years after the war's end most Japanese still do not know what the Japanese did in China. If Japan is in danger of moving toward another invasionary war and we do nothing but watch, then we can be said to be directly responsible. There is nothing to be gained from apologizing for past militarism. A true apology is to prevent the rise of militarism today.

Why Doesn't the Government Recognize the Invasion?

How is World War II viewed in Japan? The widespread understanding of the war experience is the air raids in Tokyo or the atomic bombing of Hiroshima and Nagasaki. In international peace conferences, many Japanese repeatedly invoke Hiroshima and Nagasaki. But how is it viewed by other Asians?

In the rest of Asia, the dropping of the atomic bomb represented liberation. The bomb is seen as a revenge from the heavens. Hence, it is not acceptable to invoke Hiroshima. However, most Japanese are not aware of this. There is nothing in the history textbooks that recounts what the Japanese military did.

On the fortieth anniversary of the German surrender, West German President von Weizsäcker made a memorable speech about the need to remember and recognize past war responsibility and guilt. What did the Japanese prime minister do on the fortieth anniversary of the war's end? Nakasone publicly worshipped at the Yasukuni Shrine—the shrine that honors war dead, and, in particular, war criminals—an action that earlier prime ministers had avoided. This is like going to the gravesites of important Nazi leaders in Germany. Thus, it was natural that many governments criticized the Japanese government severely. In other countries, things are different. Many European countries relentlessly and severely pursue responsibility. The same is true for Asia. In South Korea, powerful people are continuously purged. In the People's Republic of China, Mao's wife, Jiang Qing, is executed for the excesses of the Cultural Revolution. In the Philippines, the long-time dictator Marcos is forced out and vilified.

However, the Japanese government's action was predictable for those who understand the Japanese behavioral pattern. In Japan, a Class A war criminal, Kishi Nobusuke, becomes prime minister; a major war criminal like Kodama Yoshio becomes a key figure in the Lockheed scandal, and no one pursues the Emperor's war guilt. The Japanese people are irresponsible. Hence, it is to be expected and consistent that Prime Minister Nakasone should honor war criminals. Postwar conservative regimes have not changed at all; in this sense, Japan is a single-party dictatorship. In reality, nothing is different from the prewar period. The Japanese have been ruled by a single-party dictatorship since the Meiji period.

1991

Eradicating the Memory
of the Nanjing Massacre

I learned that Ishihara Shintarô, a Liberal Democratic Party member of the Diet, stated that the Nanjing massacre never occurred.

As I was writing a review of Ishihara's book, *The Japan That Can Say "No,"* I phoned Ishihara's office in order to verify the authenticity of the story. Unfortunately, Ishihara's secretary does not seem to be meticulous, because my inquiry was left unanswered. (In the early 1970s, when I wrote articles on the Nanjing massacre for *Asahi Shinbun*, which were later collected in my book, *Journey to China*, Ishihara responded quite negatively in the conservative monthly journal *Shokun!* He expressed his obvious annoyance by stating: "This is something that *Asahi Shinbun* is doing with their odd sense of mission.")

I was later able to confirm the alleged statement. The November 11, 1990, issue of *Hokkaido Shinbun* ran an article headlined "The Nanjing Massacre Was a Fiction—Chinese Americans Outraged." The article reads:

Chinese Americans are outraged by Ishihara Shintarô, a Diet member, who stated in an interview in the October issue of the American magazine, *Playboy*, that the Nanjing incident of 1937 in which the Imperial Japanese Army massacred approximately 300,000 Chinese civilians (according to the official data of the People's Republic of China) is "a story made up by the Chinese."

In response, six intellectuals sent an open letter to Ishihara, claiming that for over one hundred years prior to 1945, "the Chinese were subjected to invasions and insults by the Japanese. In the current state of history, when Sino-Japanese relations are becoming normalized, Ishihara not only refuses to face up to the historical facts but denies the Nanjing massacre. We cannot tolerate his attitude."

In the *Playboy* interview, entitled "A Bold Speech by the Number One U.S. Basher," Ishihara asserted: "People say that the Japanese made a holocaust there, but that is not true. It is a story made up by the Chinese." In response to the interviewer's queries concerning genocide, Ishihara replied: "But you dropped the atomic bombs on Japan and killed 200,000 to 300,000 people."

Ishihara, while denying any racially motivated wrongdoing on the part of the Japanese against the Chinese or others, claimed that the use of atomic bombs on Japan was the result of American racial prejudice against the Japanese: "I just said out loud the feelings that are harbored by almost all of the Japanese people. Most of us feel this in our hearts. It may be an uncomfortable message for Americans to hear."

The aforementioned open letter proclaims that the Nanjing massacre was "to the Chinese, an even more painful and more terrorizing experience" than the suffering of the Japanese caused by the atomic bombs. In an outpouring of concern and outrage, the letter states that "against such an arrogant and hasty attitude we cannot help but express our strong indignation."

The group is preparing to send its open letter demanding that Ishihara publicly apologize to the Chinese and retract his statement in *Playboy*. The members are also planning to carry an advertisement with their official proclamation of protest against Ishihara. Their plan will make possible the further widening of the debate.

The problem lies in recognizing facts. Since it would be impossible to carry out a debate based on false information, we must first confirm the relevant facts.... In claiming that the Nanjing massacre is a fiction, Ishihara is, in effect, calling the Chinese liars. But if the Nanjing massacre did take place, then Ishihara himself is a liar. Who is then the liar—Ishihara or the Chinese?

My original intention was merely to ask Ishihara whether he accepted the existence of the Nanjing atrocities. (The events in Nanjing involved not just the murder of civilians, but also repeated rape, robbery, and plunder on a mass scale. Therefore, some researchers have used the term "atrocities" rather than "massacre.") Because of my concern for facts, I have sent Ishihara the following letter of inquiry:

To Ishihara Shintarô:

Although I am neither a constituent of your district nor a member of the Liberal Democratic Party, as a believer in the right to political participation and as a taxpaying citizen, I am directing the following two questions to you. Please send me your reply within a month. Enclosed is an envelope for your reply.

1. To a question posed to you in the November 1990 issue of *Playboy*, you replied as follows: "People say that the Japanese made a holocaust there, but that is not true. It is a story made up by the

Chinese. It has tarnished the image of Japan. It is a lie." What is the basis of your statement?

2. In the same interview, you asked: "Where did Japanese people massacre?" By this, did you mean "The massacre never took place anywhere," or "I admit that the massacre did take place in certain areas"? If you meant the latter, please specify the location.

1990

$$\frac{400,000}{20,000,000} = \frac{400}{20,000} = \frac{4}{200} = \frac{1}{50}$$

Against the Logic of Invaders

Shimomura Michiko's series, "The Soviet Union's Perception of the United States," presents precious information about both the Soviet Union and the United States. Academic analyses are of course important, but excellent journalistic reports are even more important because of their larger impact. Shimomura's vigorous research is truly remarkable.

In the first article of the series, Shimomura writes:

In the Soviet Union, I met close to eighty people: party leaders, military officers, scholars, bureaucrats, writers, artists, journalists, corporate executives, religious people, workers, students, farmers.... They held similar opinions on many issues, but at the same time, there were differences that reflected their different life experiences. What impressed me was that almost everyone I spoke to stated that the crucial difference between the United States and the Soviet Union is not their ideology but whether the people had experienced war on their own land or not. The USSR experienced war on its own soil when Hitler invaded, and although it won in the end, it lost 20 million people. This casualty figure is nearly half of all the people killed in World War II. American casualties in the same period were 400,000—only 2 percent of that of the USSR. I realized that it would be difficult to comprehend the Soviet Union without being aware of the enormous casualties and sufferings that they experienced.

This crucial difference between the Soviet Union and the United States can also be applied to China and Japan. The difference in world outlook is determined not so much by ideology but by whether they have experienced an invasion. Neither Japan nor the United States have been invaded in recent history, while both China and the Soviet Union have. What does being invaded mean exactly? Of course it means destruction, but what is more devastating and significant is the impact on the home front. What exactly does invasion by an enemy force mean? In worst cases, men are killed or enslaved and women are raped. Sometimes, soldiers of the invading army go into battle solely for the sake of exercising their power over others. Conservatives frequently emphasize the existence of morally uncorrupted soldiers. Of course, there are always a few such soldiers, but their existence is only useful to those who want to justify the act of invasion. The war experience of the average Japanese was usually nothing more than the hard life on the home front—without enemy soldiers. In the last phase of World War II, many Japanese civilians were killed by massive air raids, but in the eyes of other Asians this was only divine punishment for their own war-mongering in other Asian countries. (Moreover, after the war, most of those who truly deserved divine punishment were spared.) The only part of Japan that experienced the kind of war that the Russians and the Chinese experienced is Okinawa, which lost one-third of its civilian population. (Furthermore, Okinawa was a separate kingdom that was invaded by Japan in the first place.)

In the same fashion, from the time of its independence the

United States has engaged in a series of invasions, starting with its policy of extermination toward the indigenous population. This was followed by the invasion of Mexico, Hawaii, the Philippines, Korea, and Vietnam, to name but a few. The United States was never invaded by any hostile army. To the invaded, war is horrifying and dreadful; it is the closest thing to hell. On the other hand, to the invaders, war can be romantic or a happy memory of one's youth.

The logic of the argument is self-explanatory, and the postwar generation should be able to comprehend it. For instance, the heavy price the Soviets paid for their resistance to Hitler immediately becomes clear to anyone who reads only part of *Tanya's Diary*, which describes the defense of Leningrad. However, strange as it may seem, people who take the side of the invader do not understand this reasoning very easily. Or, more accurately, they do not wish to understand it.

Unfortunately, it seems that this tendency occurs frequently in Japan, and this observation does not exclude the so-called intellectuals. Kobayashi Keiji, a reporter from the Seoul bureau of *Asahi Shinbun*, writes:

> The International PEN Congress was held in Tokyo this May. This year's theme was the abolition of nuclear weapons. One of the participants, a Korean writer, stated: "The Japanese delegates emphasize the atrocities caused by atomic bombs and speak only as war victims, while entirely ignoring Japan's responsibility for starting the war in the first place."

Needless to say, there has been no single country or ethnic group in the history of human race that has invariably been an aggressor or a victim. However, that is not the issue I am concerned with here.

I want to introduce a statement by a Byelorussian writer, Adamovich, which was in Shimomura's report:

> I once proposed that every nation should write a book—not on how much we have been victimized by aggression of other nations but on how much we as a nation have damaged other nations with our aggression. Historically, every nation has practiced violent acts against other nations, one way or another. Before the state implements disarmament, I think each nation and each ethnic group should engage in spiritual disarmament. It is relatively easy to state the truth about others, but it takes extraordinary courage for one to tell the truth about one's own nation.

Out of his belief that "only those who defenselessly experienced war possess the most accurate knowledge of the cruelty of war," Adamovich wrote *From the Flame*, based on interviews with more than three hundred survivors from several thousand villages in the Russian republic, which was invaded by the German army. He also made the following statement:

> Soldiers leave the horror of death and everything filthy in the battlefield when they come out of their trenches. As they get older, they start to remember the war of their youth fondly. After all, they experienced the war in the best period of their lives. They become romantics. However, those who never become soldiers remain realists for the rest of their lives.

After having visited and interviewed the survivors of the invasion of Nanjing, I came to the same conclusion as Adamovich. I must keep on reporting on the Nanjing massacre to fight against those unpatriotic (in the true sense of the word) journalists who continue to portray Japan's act of invasion as a "fond memory." Of course, there are a fair number of people who do understand—but they are not part of the mainstream.

It may well be that Japanese will only "understand" Adamovich's logic when the Japanese archipelago is turned into a no-man's land, which may happen if Prime Minister Nakasone keeps up his belligerent and nationalistic policy.

1984

On Platoon

I recently watched a well-regarded Hollywood movie, *Platoon*. Although it is said to be based on the experience of the second platoon of the Bravo Company of the Twenty-fifth U.S. Infantry Division, I found several questionable parts in the movie. However, I should not criticize it because it does not purport to be a documentary but rather dramatized nonfiction.

All Hollywood movies on the Vietnam war have failed to present the war from the Vietnamese perspective (the only possible exception is *Hearts and Minds*). In this regard, *Platoon* is no exception. The Vietnamese who appear briefly in the movie are depicted in an extremely inhuman and machinelike manner.

Despite these shortcomings, I want to praise the movie. It aims to expose and depict the contradictions within the U.S. military, rather than the war itself. No matter how much the U.S. military attempts to represent justice, its true purpose is to create professionally trained killers. The movie reproduces the routine massacre and rape of the Vietnamese people. A conscientious leader who attempts to prevent the violence is murdered.

More significantly, as a Japanese viewer I was impressed by the United States allowing its dirty laundry to be seen in public. Americans, in turn, endorsed it by watching the movie. The Vietnam war ended just over a decade ago [1975]. In Japan, it is still taboo half a century later to describe the Nanjing massacre or other atrocities committed by the Japanese military in China—not just in movies but also in newspapers.

A nation incapable of disclosing its shameful conduct in the past surely cannot be expected to reflect accurately or meaningfully on its history. In contemporary Japan, there are so many forces seeking to stifle such an effort in the name of patriotism.

1987

The Blindness
of Japanese Peace Movements:
Forgetting Japan's Aggression

The annual ritual in which people pray for peace, which starts on Hiroshima Day (August 6) and ends on August 15, is now over. It is expected that next year's event will be especially impressive, as it will be the fortieth anniversary of the 1945 bombing of Hiroshima and the end of World War II. It is particularly conspicuous when these events are tied to international relations in some way, but even when they have nothing to do with foreign affairs, they often appear to be nothing more than for our own gratification. No matter how much we plead for peace or a nuclear-free world, an international audience will not be convinced as long as Japanese peace movements continue to maintain such a complacent attitude.

It is a well-known fact, which I myself experienced in New York, that if you mention Hiroshima and Nagasaki in the United States, you will almost invariably hear the reply, "Remember Pearl Harbor!" Aside from the logic of this widespread reaction by the average American, at least on an emotional level, the bombing of Hiroshima is not considered an act of aggression, but rather nothing more than a reprisal to the damage inflicted by the Japanese military.

Similarly, we need to consider Asian nations that were invaded by Japan. For instance, how do South and North Koreans, who suffered the longest period of invasion by Japan, view the bombing of Hiroshima? Kim San Cho, a Korean resident of Japan, stated in "A Gathering to Discuss the Textbook Issue," which was held at Ochanomizu Women's University, that the mainstream view in Korea is that "it is only natural that atomic bombs were dropped on Japan. Our suffering was ended by the atomic bombs." The bombs are, therefore, regarded as a blessing from heaven. According to a reader's letter to *Tonga Ilbo*, a leading South Korean newspaper, the Japanese military planned to massacre 40,000 leaders of the Korean Patriotic Movement, beginning on August 17, 1945. If this is in fact true, these 40,000 people were saved by the atomic bombs.

What about the case of China? According to Yoshida Minoru of *Asahi Shinbun*, the Hong Kong movie entitled *The Testimony of the Blood* vividly describes the horror which started with the Nanjing massacre. The movie ends with the bombing of Hiroshima and Nagasaki. Yoshida observes that "for the Japanese, the use of atomic bombs is regarded as the starting point of peace and antinuclear movements, but in this movie, it is portrayed as the final settlement of the Japanese invasion of Asian countries."

No matter how vigorously the Japanese plead for Hiroshima and Nagasaki as symbols of antinuclear movements or the starting point of antiwar and peace movements, it will be impossible to arouse the sympathy of those who perceive their significance differently. For the majority of the people in Asia, their starting points are Nanjing, Singapore, Corregidor [the Philippines], Chungjing [China], Panmunjom [Korea], or countless other sites of Japanese brutality in Asia. For instance, a young journalist from Malaysia, who was invited by the Japan Newspaper Association, stated:

> I was given a briefing at the Atomic Bomb Memorial Park [in Hiroshima], but I felt that the Japanese are being unfair by only emphasizing the dropping of the atomic bombs. No word was spoken about Southeast Asia, which was tormented by the Japanese military.

A Filipino reporter said: "It is more important to tell people why the bombs were dropped. What will destroy the human race is not nuclear weapons but the social system that generates destruction." A journalist from Singapore added:

> What we were shown at Hiroshima is only one side of the story. It totally ignores the cities the Japanese military destroyed in Southeast Asia and China, emphasizes that the United States did not give warning prior to the bombing, and focuses on the debate over whether or not the dropping of a second bomb on Nagasaki can be justified.

I discussed Japan's antinuclear and peace movements with a Malaysian environmental activist immediately before August 6, the anniversary of the Hiroshima bombing. Japan is the only country to have experienced the actual effects of nuclear war, and it continues to be the main promoter of the International Symposium for the Banning of Atomic and Hydrogen Bombs, even though this organization has been manipulated and used as a tool in the domestic political power struggle. However, young people in Malaysia are disdainful even of this movement. One activist criticized the arrogance of Japan's peace movements:

Although the atomic bomb was a chance for Japan to find out the dreadfulness of nuclear weapons and the preciousness of peace, from the perspective of Southeast Asians, it was a light at the end of the tunnel, symbolizing the coming end to the atrocities committed by Japan.The Japanese military killed more than ten times the number of people in Asia than the number of victims who died from the atomic bombs dropped on Japan. Calling on other Asian peoples for solidarity in antinuclear and peace movements without remorse and without acknowledging its own atrocities in Asia will not generate support for Japan.

A similar sentiment of distrust toward Japan is common in Singapore. A historian from Singapore criticizes Japan's August 15 Day to Remember War Victims and Pray for Peace:

I think that to commemorate the spirits of 3.1 million people who became the victims of the country is a natural sentiment. But, on the other hand, 18 to 20 million people in Asia were killed by Japan's invasion. To the people in Asia, those glorified 3.1 million dead heroes were the aggressors. The people of Asia will never forget that.

Most Japanese believe the dropping of atomic bombs on Japan was an unjustifiable international act. Yet Japan used chemical weapons in China, which was prohibited by international law. However, most Japanese remain blind to our wrongdoing. If we continue to maintain this stance, not only will Japan's peace movements fail to convince, but also Japanese works of art regarding Hiroshima or its antinuclear movements will not be understood or appreciated once they leave our borders. At best, they will be understood by those countries that have never been touched by Japan's aggression and either silently ignored or met with cold laughter in other Asian countries.

A German author, Gerhard Dampmann, expressed his amazement at the difference between the treatment of war crimes committed during World War II by Japan and Germany. "The Japanese indifference regarding their war crimes damages their standing in the international community." The power of Dampmann's analysis lies in his emphasis on this very point. Although Germany conducted full-fledged investigations of its war criminals, we Japanese have never investigated our own war criminals. In short, we have not reflected on our invasion of other countries.

What can be done? The answer is obvious. Japanese peace movements must stop playing the victim role with regard to Hiroshima/Nagasaki. It is not enough for us to summon up Hiroshima after apologizing for Pearl Harbor. We must include aggression and victimization together and plead equally for Hiroshima, Auschwitz, and Nanjing. For ordinary citizens were surely victims in every country.

However, words alone are not enough to build trust. Simply speaking about and displaying both aspects will have limited power to convince people that we are truly remorseful about our role in World War II. Evidence of this remorse must be clearly manifested in our attitude and actions. The most convincing evidence is the investigation of war criminals carried out by Germany and Italy. As Dampmann points out, a country in which certain people continue to hold power even after causing so much suffering (both to their own people and to the people of other nations) is "truly rare" in history. Reflecting this reality, even Japanese literature and drama are more superficial than those of Germany. A Finn residing in Japan criticizes Japanese insistence on seeing itself only as a victim. He claims that he cannot disclose his name for fear of social sanctions:

> Don't mention my name. In West Germany, for instance, criticizing Germany for its war crimes is socially accepted, so I would never worry about disclosing my name for doing so. This is natural in Germany, where sites of atrocities have been turned into museums and memorials. However, if I openly criticize Japanese war crimes in Japan, it would jeopardize my employment.

He adds that not being able to disclose one's identity is deeply symbolic of the problem.

Granting this fact, the first step is to deepen the recognition that Japan was an aggressor. Although it would be almost hopelessly difficult to achieve reforms capable of transforming the consciousness of a nation, true patriotism is the complete opposite of the commercialized "patriotism" practiced by the Japanese right wing. We must take it one step at a time.

1984

The Burden of Being Japanese

As I was about to write a review of Ralph Giordano's *The Second Crime: The Burden of Being German* [*Die Zweite Schuld oder von der Last Deutscher zu Sein*], two television programs made me realize that a long introduction was necessary. But before I discuss the programs, I want to begin with a symbolic incident that occurred in the annual remembrance of Hiroshima and Nagasaki on August 15, the same day forty-six years ago when Japan surrendered unconditionally and World War II finally ended.

The Korean Memorial Tombstone Incident

Immediately after I left for Germany to report on German reunification, I read an article in *Asahi Shinbun* entitled "Why Isn't the Memorial Tombstone Allowed Inside the Park: The Korean Victims of the Bomb Outraged":

On April 16, thirteen members of the Association of the Korean Victims of the Atomic Bomb (headquartered in Seoul), led by chairman Sin Yông Su, visited the tombstone of the atomic bomb victims located inside the Peace Park in Hiroshima. When the party discovered that the tombstone of the Korean victims is located outside the park, they were outraged. The members protested: "The Japanese discriminate not only against living Koreans but also dead Koreans!" and pounded the tombstone with their fists.

The tombstone was constructed in 1970 by the Hiroshima chapter of the Korean Residents Association in Japan. It is 5 meters high and is set on a large base shaped like a turtle. In 1967, there were already too many tombstones inside the park. The association constructed a tombstone for the Korean victims in the present location after reaching an agreement with the city, which forbade new tombstones inside the park.

After visiting and praying in front of the tombstones inside the park, the party placed a bouquet by the tombstone for the Korean victims. As Chairman Sin stated: "The fact that the tombstone was not allowed in the park clearly shows that we Koreans are discriminated against even after our death." Several members began to weep and pounded the base of the tombstone with their fists and shouted in Korean: "This is horrible! Don't discriminate against us!"

The party then went on to meet Deputy Mayor Fukushima Takayoshi at the Hiroshima City Hall and demanded that the tombstone be moved inside the park. The deputy mayor, in typical Japanese bureaucratic fashion, responded: "We consider this matter to be serious. However, I'm afraid that we cannot decide on the issue immediately." He avoided making a clear commitment. Angry voices were raised against Araki Takeru, the mayor of Hiroshima, who did not meet with the party, claiming that he had a prior appointment: "While the mayor of Nagasaki apologized to us by saying 'We regret that we have troubled you for a long time,' it is quite disappointing that the mayor of Hiroshima does not even meet with us."

In this manner, the relocation of the memorial tombstone of the Korean victims came to public attention. As a matter of fact, this wasn't the first time it was made into an issue. Five years after it was built [1975], a request was made to the city to move the tombstone inside the park, but the city has continued to deny the request for the same reason reported in the article.

On April 20, the chairman of the Liaison Committee of the Korean Atomic Bomb Victims in Japan held a press conference at Hiroshima City Hall. He asked, "Isn't it only right for the Japanese to construct a memorial tombstone dedicated to all the victims of the atomic bomb, including Koreans, inside the park?" Furthermore, on May 18, the chairman of the Central Headquarters of the Korean Residents Association in Japan visited the Hiroshima City Hall and requested the relocation of the tombstone. The city promised that it would move the tombstone into the park by August 6 [the day of the bombing] on condition that the tombstone be one that represented both South and North Koreans. However, a little after 1 a.m. on May 23, the day before the arrival of South Korean President Roh Tae Woo, arsonists damaged the tombstone, and folded paper cranes [symbol of peace] and poems written on fancy paper [a Japanese goodwill custom] were burned. This is not the first such incident. In fact, this was the third time.

On June 18, a group of activists and scholars set up a preparation committee for the relocation of the tombstone. One of the members, Toyonaga Eizaburô, the head teacher of the high school branch of Hiroshima Electric Engineering College and a longtime supporter of the Korean victims of the atomic bomb, stated: "I think it is more important for us to build a tombstone to apologize for the crimes Japan committed against Koreans than a tombstone to commemorate Korean victims representing both sides [South and North]." However, the "memorial tombstone of apology" never materialized; no statement of Japan's aggression against Korea would be carved out on the tombstone.

The League of Koreans in Japan (sympathetic to North Korea), the Korean Residents Association in Japan (sympathetic to South Korea), and other Japanese citizens' organizations protested loudly. The head of the Hiroshima Korean Residents Association in Japan stated: "The historical fact of Japan's mass-scale forced abduction of Koreans during the World War II will be erased from memory.... Are we going to allow them to trample on our history?" In the end, it was decided that the relocation by August 6 was impossible.

The German Recognition of Aggression and War Crime Museums

What is the situation in Germany—a nation whose behavior was similar to that of Japan in terms of having engaged in merciless invasion of neighboring nations? How have East and West Germany dealt with the history of aggression since 1945? How do they demonstrate their remorse over their wartime activities? I was able to visit museums in both West and East Germany.

First, I will discuss West Germany. I don't know the precise number of museums, but they are spread all over the country, and most of them are large. The memorial museum that was built in the city of Nanjing five years ago [1985] is large, but it was built by the Chinese—the victims of the atrocity. However, in the case of both West and East Germany, their museums were all built by themselves—the aggressors. The museums in Germany—the German equivalent of the Hiroshima tombstone—are larger than the one in Nanjing. I visited the Bergen-Belsen concentration camp, located close to the East German border. Buses of tourists and many private cars indicated that the museum had many visitors. At the entrance, there are greetings in German, Hebrew, and English. Inside the museum, the workings of the concentration camp were explained with vivid photographs and numerous data, graphs, and other materials. Information, such as where the victims came from, can be gleaned easily. Books summarizing these facts are also on sale. Behind the museum, a huge ruin of the former concentration camp is preserved as a park and a cemetery. There are many tombstones, with epigraphs like "Here lie 2,500 dead," or "Here lie 1,000 dead." When the British military liberated and occupied this camp, they conducted burials using captured German personnel. Also there is a separate memorial tombstone, dedicated to the 30,000 Jewish victims who perished in this camp. The memorial tombstone consists of a huge tower about 30 meters high, with a tall, stout wall behind it. Various words of protest are carved on the wall in the languages of the victims, and the base of the tower and the wall are full of flowers brought by visitors.

How about East Germany? It has also preserved sites and museums. For an example of a smaller monument I visited a forced labor camp which is located near the southern border with West Germany. The camp held mainly Russians and Poles. Just before the end of the war, those deemed "useless" were forced into a cave and buried alive; the entrance to the cave was sealed with explosives. After the war, the site was converted into a memorial mall so that visitors can tour the site as they stroll through a wood of spruce, horse chestnut, and lime trees.

As an example of a large monument, I visited Buchenwald in Weimar. Weimar is famous for the Weimar constitution and as the cultural home of Goethe and Schiller. There are beech trees [*Buchenwald*] on the hill located on the north-western outskirts of Weimar. Nazi Germany cut down the trees and built an immense forced-labor camp. Of approximately 250,000 prisoners, about 65,000 died. Especially horrifying was the case of the Russian prisoners—8,483 were shot to death and disposed of in the incinerator.

This memorial park is even larger than its counterpart in West Germany. It is perhaps twenty times the size of the memorial hall in Nanjing. It is so vast that I had to visit the facility twice to see it in its entirety. The site is divided into two large sections: one contains the site of the forced-labor camp and the memorial hall, and the other consists of numerous memorial tombstones which are placed around three gigantic cemeteries. At the gate of the camp, there are prisoners' barracks and forced-labor factories. There are tombstones here and there among the ruins. Epitaphs are carved in the various languages of the victims. In the corner opposite the gate, there is a three-story museum which displays the workings of the camp, using photographs and replicas. Whether or not this is characteristically German, I do not know, but they reproduced everything with utmost thoroughness.

Between the museum and the gate there is an incinerator,

and a slaughter-house is located to the east. This is perhaps the most ghastly corner of all. In the first room, the prisoners were given a so-called physical examination. In the next room, there is a vertical scale for measuring height; on it there is a rectangular hole at approximately the level of the nape of the neck. As the prisoner turned his back to the scale on the wall, a staff person in charge of slaughter shot him through the hole. The bodies whose height had been "measured" were sent to the basement of the incinerator on a truck. From the basement, the cargo elevator moved the bodies to the incineration chamber.

Many young Russians who were murdered at this camp have been identified by their parents and relatives, who have visited the camp and left small monuments with brief words of farewell to their beloved sons and brothers. The words, carved in small boards, express their inexpressible sorrow. These boards reminded me of the comments typically heard in Japan, such as "the tragedy of war" or "never war again." It would be interesting to study when this "consensus" was arrived at, but I hypothesize that the mass media played a role in manufacturing it. For instance, at least in the past, whether a particular article was accepted was determined by its political implications. If the author blamed "war" itself for causing all the tragedies of war, her or his contribution was likely to be accepted. If the author blamed the act of invasion for creating social misery, her or his contribution was likely to be rejected. Every year, as August 15 approaches, we hear clichés about the tragedy of war but they are devoid of meaning and merely conceal Japanese war crimes. The truth is that we invaded other countries, and therein lies our crime. To speak of war only expunges all history and context and significance.

Buchenwald is located on a hill three hundred meters above Weimar. There is a cemetery for the Buchenwald victims on the slope that faces Weimar, and it too has been turned into a colossal memorial park. The path inside the park descends from the driveway to the forced-labor camp and eventually leads back to the driveway; and it is perhaps more than one kilometer long. There are many monuments placed along the pathway. First there is a huge bell tower fifty meters high. Three cemeteries shaped in the form of a coliseum are connected by eighteen pylons with engravings to mark the eighteen European nations the victims came from, including France, Poland, and Czechoslovakia. Lastly, there are statues of eleven heroic victims denoting their determination to fight fascism. I felt nothing but admiration and astonishment at those monuments and the sheer size of the memorial parks.

Such extensive memorial facilities expressing the Germans' "grave reflection on their aggression" exist in both West and East Germany, and they are crowded with visitors every day. For travelers from Japan, an aggressor nation in Asia, visits to the Buchenwald or Bergen-Belsen memorials, built by another former aggressor, Germany, will provide much to think about—more so than visits to Auschwitz, which has been preserved in Poland by the Polish, who were the victims of war.

The Relationship Between Hiroshima and a Novelist

At the beginning of this essay, I mentioned two television programs. One of them was "Does the World Still Remember

Hiroshima? Journey of Dialogue and Contemplation with Oe Kenzaburô." As its title suggests, the program was written and produced by Oe himself and is designed to reflect on Hiroshima, which was subjected to the world's first use of the atomic bomb. Oe produced the program by intermingling interviews he conducted with intellectuals from the Soviet Union and the United States with scenes from his private and family life. The program begins with a scene in which Oe's son is writing a piece of music motivated by the tragedy of Hiroshima; it ends with the performance of the completed piece and Oe's personal reflection. Eight people are interviewed, including nuclear physicists and novelists in the USSR and the United States, one of whom is Asian. (Besides the survivors of Hiroshima, there are other victims of nuclear weapons throughout the world, such as the native peoples of the South Pacific islands and Australia, but intellectuals from these areas are not included in the program.)

The one Asian is a Korean poet, Kim Chi Ha. Kim's response to Hiroshima is totally different from that of the other interviewees:

> *Kim:* First of all, I think that the title of this program is misleading. We should be asking; "Does the world still remember 300,000 people who were massacred in Nanjing?" or "Do we still remember 1 million Asians who were victims of World War II?" or "Do we still remember Koreans who were forcibly taken to be used as expendable workers?" or "Do we still remember Koreans who were victimized by atomic bombs?" Even though Japan attempts to play a major role in Asia, unless it comes to terms with all the historical errors made in the past and makes it clear that it is no longer tainted, Japan won't be qualified to participate, not only in the future of Asia but in the future of the world as well. Before pleading to the world, "Do you still remember Hiroshima?" the Japanese people need to answer

the aforementioned questions and organize the movement to re-deem the crimes Japan committed in the past.

Oe: If done my way, reflection on the question, "Does the world still remember Hiroshima?" would lead to a critique based on moral and ethical grounds. The program's point of departure is our desire to contemplate issues like: "Do we still remember these things?" "In this world, is Hiroshima still being remembered?" "Does Japan, as a member of the world community, still remember Hiroshima?" We have not completely made up for what we have done, and I think that I am responsible for myself and the crimes of Japan. And through my life's work, literature, I can fulfill that responsibility and carry out such a mission. We who are on our father's side should take responsibility for things our fathers and grandfathers did at our age. We are tainted, and as tainted human beings we must discover whether or not a new ethical path can be found for the Japanese people—and that is why I am doing this television program.

Did Oe's program answer the questions Kim asked? Most interviews never discussed Kim's questions. Oe himself neither raised such issues nor asked questions regarding Japanese war crimes. There is virtually nothing new in Oe's program except that his son appears in it.

Of course, to say that nothing is new does not mean that it is valueless. Important topics should be repeated many times. However, that is not the case here.

I believe that Kim's questions justified Oe's television program. But did Oe produce the program to introduce the Japanese people to Kim's questions? That is impossible. If that were the case, the program would have been completely different. Kim's statement was not planned—it was beyond Oe's imagination, it shook the foundation of Oe's way of life. What is striking is Kim's confidence when he saw Oe's surprised look. To Oe's response, Kim spoke with a smile:

I believe that building an appeal around Hiroshima will ultimately solve a variety of problems, and Japan's various crimes will vanish in time. Further, we must eliminate nuclear weapons from Japan, Korea, and the rest of the world. I hope that in both countries the antinuclear movement will become more active. However, above all, I hope that Japan will come to terms with its past wrongdoing and show the rest of the world that it is morally pure.

Kim was being kind; to appeal as victims and about Hiroshima will never erase Japanese crimes. To say that he believes Oe's contradictory response is the reverse of saying that he cannot comprehend Oe but will believe him out of sympathy.

Of course, Oe understands the surface meaning of Kim's questions. Therefore, after the interview Oe let the narrator speak for him: "I must deal with Kim's criticism of the Japanese people as a critique of what I have been doing and what I will be doing. Furthermore, it is a critique that young Japanese people will have to face head on."

Oe plays a sleight of hand here. After generalizing Kim's criticism of his program into a criticism of all Japanese, he makes himself look good by saying that he will "deal with" what he has been doing. Those who need to face the critique head on are not young people but older people, especially people like Oe himself. How can younger people "deal with" the criticism when older people are running away?

Oe's method of self-promotion is never to disturb the status quo. He always makes sure that neither the right nor the left will attack him, that he will not be disliked by major broadcasting stations or publishers. Oe never displays courage. It would be one thing if he were an ordinary novelist, but he is someone who claims to think seriously about humanity's pressing problems and puts himself forward as an anti-establishment novelist. To borrow the critic Okaniwa Noboru's language, Oe is a "'progressive' writer who loves the status quo" and "works for the establishment." He clings to the mystique of the progressive intellectuals that stems from the late 1960s and early 1970s.

The most important aspect of the nuclear issue in contemporary Japan is undoubtedly nuclear power plants. However, Oe never upsets large capitalists with stakes in nuclear power or their lackey media people. I can only take my hat off to the many unknown people who have fought and struggled against nuclear power, but I keep my hat on for Oe. It would be a "waste" for Oe to involve himself in grassroots movements that disturb the status quo—that would not be "working for the establishment."

There are two fundamentally different ways to look at Hiroshima and Nagasaki: (1) as a direct result of our aggression, or (2) as a step toward the destruction of humanity. Previously, almost all Japanese have focused on the second perspective; the first was missing. Even though the two are different, unfortunately they stem from the same event. Hence, the greatest aggressor for many Asian countries, Japan, could present itself as the victim and appeal from the second perspective.

Both perspectives are important, but it is imperative to process the first. As long as the second perspective is the only one that concerns him, no one will become angry at Oe; it is of no concern to the right wing. It is like praying for world peace. However, if he should start tackling the first....

Of course, we cannot but mourn the victims of atomic bombs or Tokyo air raids. But the anger must be aimed at both the inhuman United States, which killed ordinary citizens without any warning, and at the Japanese criminals, who initiated the war.

Let's clarify the distinction between the two perspectives. First, if Nazi Germany had perfected nuclear weapons before the United States and used them on Moscow or London, then no one could deny German aggression. Further, the citizens of Moscow or London could exclusively focus on their victimization as the first step in the destruction of humanity. In this scenario, Nazi Germany could monopolize the guilt and the people of the Soviet Union or Britain could concentrate on the "problem concerning humanity."

Second, what if Germany had appealed to the world about the tragic fate of Germany? No doubt the heavy bombing in Dresden and other battles in Germany wreaked havoc. It is estimated that about 7 million Germans died in the World War II. However, if Germans ignore the damage wrought by their aggression, would it be in any way persuasive to discuss the tragedies of Dresden or Berlin? However, the way in which Japan appeals to the world about Hiroshima and Nagasaki is roughly the same as in this scenario.

Third, in 1937, there was an attack on Japanese soldiers east of Beijing. In the newspaper of the day, this incident made the headlines. *Asahi Shinbun*, for example, wrote of the "massacre of innocent Japanese." However, this massacre deep inside Chinese territory was the result of Japanese aggression. How persuasive is it to discuss the atrocity committed by the Chinese people? Isn't this like Hiroshima?

What Prompted Her to Speak?

The second television program was entitled "The Mobilization of Nagoya Female High School Students." Toward the end of the war many female high school students had been mobilized to work in a fighter plane factory in Nagoya. At a recent reunion, they staged a play and the program was about this play.

One of the newscasters was a young Korean-Japanese woman. She interviewed one of the former students—a Korean woman named Kim who now lives in Cheju-do, South Korea.

The interview was moving. Before the war began, Kim had come to study in Japan; although she was fourteen, she was forced to work in a Mitsubishi factory. She was beaten for being ten minutes late to work, and she suffered many hardships. Her husband had a thirteen-year-old sister who was also mobilized to work and died in a factory accident. "For whom?" cried the husband. "She died like a dog."

After this, other high school students appear and gather around the Zero Fighter Plane that they worked to produce during the war. They become nostalgic as they think about the young men who died on the planes they made. One woman tells the Korean-Japanese newscaster:

> It would seem today that we were aiding the war effort but that's not so, we were seriously working for the country. In any case, the Zero plane was so light, it seemed clear that we were building suicide machines.

> It's sad, but there is nothing I could have done. In order to value everyone's life, it seems important to take care of this small fighter plane as a symbol of the tragedy of war.

The program then shifts to contemporary Nagoya, where F-15 fighter planes are built by Mitsubishi Heavy Industries and "ordinary" workers commute to the factory.

After the program, I interviewed one of the former students. She learned about Korean people's suffering for the first time: "We saw that and we became disgusted. We were naive. We said that we experienced war, but we were privileged as female high school students. We don't usually think of the war but we thought it over and developed some self-hatred. Compared to them, we are embarrassing."

These women began to understand the soul of the invaded after forty-five years. That is to say, they didn't understand it before. Although they thought about the young Japanese men who died in "suicide planes," they could not think about the people who were attacked by these same planes. The program taught them the victim's viewpoint.

But what surprised me was the afterword by the Korean-Japanese newscaster. "I used to think that the Japanese could only be seen as aggressors. This time I heard so many stories of how these women were brought over in their youth and unknowingly built fighter planes. Of course, it's terrible to make young people do it, but it seems that these women were victims because they were forced to do it without knowing about it."

I could understand what she was saying up to this point. What really surprised me was the conclusion: "From listening to various stories by Japanese people, I realized that war itself is at fault; it's not really a matter of who are the aggressors and who are the victims."

I felt like I had been hit in the face. Such a conclusion by a Korean Japanese! I heard later that this young woman used her Korean name despite the opposition of her parents.* In a subsequent interview with Chi Myong Kwan of Tokyo Women's University, I explored the issue further.

> *Honda:* The Japanese mass media has traditionally used the concept "all war is bad" to avoid assuming responsibility for Japanese war crimes, but I was surprised to hear a Korean-Japanese woman say that.

> *Chi:* Perhaps she was concerned about her Japanese acquaintances. She was probably thinking of her audience, and she wanted to warn them about what war would mean. However, she didn't want to say that the Japanese were guilty—out of her goodness of heart. Also, it may be that her personal relations with Japanese are good. Talented Korean-Japanese in a favorable environment probably won't be too critical, as people tend to treat them well. I think this is particularly true for female students. I recently went to the United States. While Korean male students were radical and critical of America, many female students were saying, "Everyone can be friends." This woman might be such a person. In terms of everyday experience, she may not think of war crimes or invasions, but this attitude may change in a political debate. At my university, there are exchange students from Korea. Usually, they are very friendly, but when they discuss political problems, they change and become hostile.

> *Honda:* The television broadcaster may be the same, given that she appeared against her parents' wishes.

> *Chi:* In her case, she would probably have answered more forth-rightly if it were the problem of Korean Japanese or of war responsibility.

---

* In Japan, most Korean Japanese use Japanese names in order to "pass" as Japanese. Because Japanese citizenship is primarily based on blood ties, it is difficult for most Korean Japanese to become naturalized citizens. See "The Discriminated Fingers," *Monthly Review* 38 (1987).

Honda: So it's not that she doesn't know; she knows but doesn't want to say it.

Chi: I would think so. Furthermore, in Korea there is no tradition of revenge, especially in interpersonal relations. She is perhaps following this tradition. Koreans tend to generalize what happens to them as fate; one's suffering turns into a philosophy. Thus, although it's possible to criticize Japanese in general, interpersonal relations remain close. Koreans tend to concern themselves with general theories rather than concrete individuals. There is no tradition like the Japanese one in which revenge is considered a virtue.

The Second Crime

This is the prologue to my review of *The Second Crime* by Ralph Giordano. Reading this book, an ordinary Japanese would not understand the meaning of the title, but might end up instead grossly misinterpreting it along the lines of "Germany is just like Japan." To understand the book, one must ask oneself: "What about Japan?" Giordano writes of how Germany lost militarily but not ideologically. In Japan the defeat ended the imperial military state, and some war criminals were executed. However, although Hitler and the Nazi flag disappeared from Germany, the symbol of invasion, the Emperor, and the Japanese flag and national anthem continue unaltered in Japan. And as with the case of Kishi Nobusuke, there is an essential continuity from the prewar period.[*]

---

[*] As Honda repeatedly stresses, Kishi was one of the most serious war criminals but went on to serve as prime minister in the late 1950s.

According to Giordano, the "first crime" is the crime of invasion and murder by the Germans under the Hitler regime. The "second crime" is the psychological repression of the first crime. Although Giordano is critical of present-day Germans, they do attempt to educate the next generation accurately about the facts of the invasions and the perspectives of the victims of German aggression. What about Japan? As we can see from the controversy over textbooks, "invasion" becomes "advance," while there is an effort to deny the Nanjing massacre. Both the Ministry of Education and the courts are doing their best to distort the perspective of the future generation. Even before people who committed the first crime have died off, the distortion campaign is nearly complete in Japan.

When I was in elementary school during the war, I heard many stories from soldiers about killing the Chinese with their swords or splitting human beings by tying their legs to horses running in opposite directions. However, in the postwar period, such stories have been confined to veterans' drinking parties. Of course, there are genuinely patriotic Japanese soldiers who tell true stories of horror, but they are the exception. Furthermore, even those who speak of their war crimes rarely discuss the most embarrassing acts, such as rape.

In Germany, there are many sites to mark their war guilt and to remember and educate new generations. But Giordano believes that these efforts are inadequate. However, in Japan, there is no museum to mark Japanese war crimes. Usually, the establishment focuses on victimization; the exceptions are few and far between.

Giordano accuses Germans of dissembling about their

past. However, their "big lies" are nothing compared to their Japanese counterparts. Almost no one in Germany denies Buchenwald or Bergen-Belsen or Auschwitz. In Japan, a Diet member like Ishihara publicly denies the Nanjing massacre although its historical veracity has been confirmed repeatedly. Such a state of affairs is not possible in Germany.

In Japan, the situation is dire. People who "lie" and "manufacture stories" are not those who deny Japanese war guilt but people like me. Professor Watanabe Shôichi, for example, completely denies the Nanjing massacre and claims that my efforts to substantiate the facts are tantamount to lying to our children. There are "Watanabe Shôichi" everywhere, who would insist on the flatness of the earth in spite of overwhelming evidence to the contrary. What is unique about Japan is that such a charlatan can appear in mainstream newspapers and on television programs. This is not possible in Germany.

In Japan, "postwar democracy," albeit with pressure from the U.S. occupation force, led to land reform and the purge of wartime politicians. It also ushered in a period when the people overturned the prewar value system. Many Japanese "intellectuals"—even cowards—rode that wave to write "courageous" criticisms and "brave" novels. However, after the Vietnam war and especially with the mounting contradictions of the Eastern bloc countries, Japanese intellectuals began to side with the establishment. The previously "courageous" writers began to transform themselves: "wise" people became silent, clever people began to fool readers with their "ambivalence," while the unprincipled simply became reactionary.

Giordano discusses how Germans, although they inflicted considerable damage, also experienced defeat and victimization. This is clearly different from Japan. Germany became the site of many battles; German hardship during and after the war was considerable. However, Japan was protected by the United States. Japan, except for Okinawa, was never invaded. In effect, Japan was never punched back.

Japan only regrets war, but not invasion. Japan only discusses Hiroshima to accentuate its victimization. Our road should be clear. As Giordano writes of the first crime of our grandparents and parents, we are in the process of committing the second crime. "We" in this sense includes people like Oe and me, who grew up under the militarist regime. What we did not resolve will fall on the shoulders of the next generation, and they will become the perpetrators of the second crime.

Giordano also writes about the process of alleviating war crime. From qualitative assessment of guilt, there are efforts to lessen the actual number of victims of the Holocaust, for example. Eventually, the original figure of 6 million is reduced by thousands, hundreds of thousands, and even millions. Similarly, in Japan, people carp at figures. With a lower figure, the crime is no longer considered "serious." But the essential problem is that there is no sympathy with the victims, as Giordano points out. All the effort is put into combatting the figures of atrocity, rather than regretting the fact of invasion and war crimes.

In the case of Japan, people like Ishihara Shintarô, Oe Kenzaburô, or myself, who came of age during the Fifteen Years' War, cannot be directly responsible for the first crime. However, when Ishihara denies the Nanjing massacre, he is responsible for the second crime. Also, people like Oe, who writes for the publisher that supports Ishihara—like many who vote for Ishihara—are also partially responsible for the second crime.*

Our generation has no obligation to apologize to the people for the Japanese invasion. However, we must recognize Japanese war guilt. We must not let the prewar symbol of militarism re-emerge or let the prime minister revive Yasukuni Shrine as a public institution. As long as we let these things go on, we become responsible, and pass on our crime to our children's generation.

The third postwar generation in Japan is going abroad in a manner unimaginable in Japan a few years back. It is common for young Japanese people to visit nearby Asian countries. However, in these countries there are people who detest our national anthem and flag. How many Japanese youth are aware of the reason for their hatred? Many Japanese are ignorant and merely enjoy the high value of the yen—this is the result of our second crime.

The Second Crime will be read differently by different people. There are French as well as Russian readings. Similarly, what I have been writing is from the Japanese perspective. Furthermore, I write not abstractly as an ordinary Japanese but from my personal concrete perspective. This is not the same perspective as the French or Russians. *The Second Crime* is of interest and importance not only to Germans but to Japanese as well, I think.

Among critics of *The Second Crime*, there are those who point out that Giordano's mother is Jewish and explain his analysis in terms of his "Jewishness." In the process, the book

---

* Honda refers to Bungei Shunjû, the right-wing publisher instrumental in renouncing Japanese war responsibility and guilt.

becomes devoid of universality and seemingly of interest only to other Jews. However, *The Autobiography of Malcolm X* is not only of interest to African Americans, and a book on the Ainu is not only of interest to the Ainu people in Japan. The problem is not of individual motivation but rather whether the result has universality or not, whether there is an appeal that goes beyond national borders and specific groups. Great thoughts always begin from concrete personal situations and backgrounds. *The Second Crime*, whether intended or not by Giordano, has profound appeal beyond Germany.

1991

II
Racism and Neocolonialism in Contemporary Japan

Racist Country, Japan

"Japanese like to claim that 'Unlike white people, we don't have prejudice against black people,'" wrote a black college teacher in Japan. Exactly, I thought. I wrote an article two years ago on the racist treatment of black students in Japan. About 80 percent of the responses expressed apologies. However, nearly half the apologies claimed that only some Japanese are racist; the majority are, according to these people, not racists.

Is that really the case? The black college teacher wrote that he had difficulty finding housing and also experienced racism at work. There are other corroborating stories. One of my female acquaintances was told by her landlord that her boyfriend, who is a black American, could no longer visit the apartment, so she went to look for a new place. When she found a suitable apartment, she told the real estate agent that she had an American fiancé. His response was, "Is he white or black?" Although the question irked her, she was desperate and said that he was white. However, the realtor called the landlord, who turned her down. My acquaintance only found an apartment with her fifth real estate agent.

I asked a close acquaintance who is a realtor about the situation. He said that in general it was true that blacks were disliked. Another friend, a journalist claiming to be a Korean Japanese, attempted to rent an apartment. All the vacancies were filled. In some apartments, there was a poster saying, "Only Japanese Allowed." This is exactly what happened before the war in order to keep Koreans and Okinawans out. And exactly the same sentiment lives on. Last year, a realtor said, "There are good Koreans, but rental values go down if there are Koreans in the neighborhood."

The common sense of realtors and apartment managers is ultimately the common sense of the vast majority of Japanese. The claim that only a minority of Japanese are racist would be destroyed by experiencing one day as a black person in Japan.

In Ralph Ellison's words, the oppressed are invisible to those who discriminate. Just as the oppressed of the United States exploded, the ugly reality of Japanese racism will become more evident as more blacks come to Japan and the number of low-wage workers from Southeast Asia increases in the future.

1973

Black Students in Japan

Blacks who come to Japan as students—not as soldiers, entertainers, or diplomats—are few. Racial discrimination against blacks in the United States and South Africa is well known, but what about Japan? I put this question to African American students who have been studying at Jôchi University in Tokyo. In summary, they will be going home "feeling very disappointed with Japan." From what I have heard, including from Africans, this is unfortunately the typical experience of Japan for most black people.

A male (black) student and two female students (one black, one white) agreed to "testify" about Japanese discrimination against blacks. All three came from California to study Japanese culture:

Account 1. One time, two black students visited a black professional wrestler staying at a hotel. They tried to catch a taxi at the gate of the hotel, but no matter how much they waved their arms, the taxis invariably passed them, only to pick up white customers who were standing right next to them. Some of the white customers even said to the students and the wrestler, "You were first in line. Please go ahead." When this happened, however, the taxi drivers would shut the door and drive away. This happened three times in a row. As this is a normal phenomenon in Japan, the students were not surprised. The professional wrestler, however, was shocked and enraged. Until that time, the wrestler had received special treatment because he was an entertainer. He became aware of the reality of discrimination in Japan for the first time when he went out with "ordinary blacks."

Account 2. A white female student was working at a church as an English teacher. One day when she was unable to make it to her class, she asked her roommate (who is black) to teach the class for her. As soon as her supervisor, a middle-aged Japanese woman, saw the roommate, she exclaimed, "*You* are going to teach?" The expression on the supervisor's face showed less surprise than contempt. She asked the roommate, "Where did *you* come from?" The roommate responded that she was an American from California. "But *originally* where did you come from?" asked the supervisor. At the time, the roommate wondered where the supervisor's ancestors had come from. Another thought which crossed her mind was, "Maybe this woman wants me to say that my ancestors came to America from Africa in slave ships. But does she know of the widely accepted academic theory that the origin of all human beings can be traced to Africa?" While they were talking, the time at which the class was scheduled to begin passed. The supervisor, despite the fact that she had started the conversation, complained that the roommate was late.

These are not isolated examples of Japanese racism; in fact, there are countless others. Black students can only relax while they are in their own rooms because discrimination is an everyday occurrence in Japan. When a white GI gets drunk and makes a scene, the Japanese people say, "The GI is getting drunk!" But if it is a black GI, they think, "The black is getting drunk!!" Such is the viewpoint of the average Japanese. Even when it comes to private matters, the male student finds it difficult to escape from racially motivated harassment. For example, when he is taking a shower in the dormitory, he hears voices coming from the direction of the large bathtub [traditional public bath]: "If he comes into the tub, won't the water turn black?"

Certainly there is an element of curiosity in the way in which blacks are treated. However, would an adult Japanese directly point out a white person in the subway or touch his or her hair? The black female student observes that Japanese prejudice is manifested in the ways in which they express their curiosity. Whether it is a stereotype about blacks or whites, the Japanese people have been brainwashed by the perspective of the white world.

At one time, the white female student was teaching English to office workers in a bank. Once, she introduced her roommate to one of the male office workers. Confused after finding out that her roommate was a black woman, he asked the white woman, "How am I supposed to treat her? Should I treat her like a servant, or should I treat her in the same way a Japanese would treat a Korean?" In this way, the white student inadvertently found out that this office worker also harbored extreme racial prejudice against Koreans.

The black male student said that he came to Japan for his overseas study because he wanted to get away from his own country. As long as he was going abroad, he thought, "Why not go to Japan, a civilized country of fellow people of color, where my yellow brothers live." "Later," he recounts, "I learned the bitter truth—that believing the Japanese people were my brothers was an illusion." He concluded:

> I never knew how strangely we were viewed or how thick was the wall of discrimination against blacks in Japan. Japan is not an easy

country for any foreigner to live in, but for black people there is the added burden of horrendous discrimination. This is more than disappointing—it is appalling. On the list of the world's most racially prejudiced nations, shouldn't Japan be placed next to South Africa and the United States?

1971

The Situation of the Ainu People

Every summer, Hokkaido becomes a popular vacation spot for students and tourists. In trains, we see posters of Hokkaido. Inevitably, there are pictures of *ekashi* [elderly] Ainu people in these posters. Sometimes, there are young girls playing *mukkuri* [a traditional Ainu harp-like instrument]. In fact, there are many pre-packaged tours to the Ainu areas. However, tourists never come to comprehend the situation of the Ainu people during their Hokkaido trip.

There is no doubt that the Yamato people [ethnic Japanese] were not the original inhabitants of Hokkaido. Historically, and until very recently, Hokkaido was called Ainu-moshiri [the land of the Ainu people]. How did it become "Hokkaido"? In short, the Tokugawa *bakufu* and the Meiji government, in concert with private interests, swindled its original inhabitants out of their land.

Did the swindle occur a long time ago? Was it all finished by the Meiji period? In fact, the tragedy continues. I want to introduce a recent example.

The Hidaka area has many Ainu residents and is well known for its horse ranches. In one town lived an elderly Ainu couple. Their daughters had married and moved away; they did not have a son. Fourteen years ago, the husband died in a traffic accident. The elderly woman was alone in her house but she owned two parcels of land. She was forced to sell one lot, which was contiguous to a large ranch owner. A friendly *shamo* [the Ainu word for Japanese] proposed to take care of the other lot, and the elderly woman gratefully accepted this offer. She earned enough money as a cook to support herself. However, four or five years ago she wanted to retire and live off her land. Because the "friendly" Japanese was paying only a minimal sum, she wanted to rent the land to someone who was willing to pay more. However, the Japanese told her that he had bought the land and her house as well. Unbeknownst to the elderly woman, she had been swindled out of her property by the "friendly" Japanese.

Someone who learned of this story became angry and attempted to file a lawsuit. However, the customs of rural society are not so simple. Even if the elderly Ainu woman won the lawsuit, it is clear that she would suffer from daily harassment. Hence, the woman did not want to press the suit. The problem was "solved." This is no different from what happened to Ainu land in the Tokugawa period. This is the situation of the oppressed Ainu people.

1974

The Last Appeal
of the Ainu People

The Nibutani area in the Hidaka region of Hokkaido has the most dense concentration of Ainu in Japan. This area runs from the peaks of the Hidaka mountains to the Saru River. Salmon and other riches of the sea are plentiful. And it is one of the most significant sites of Ainu mythology.

Today, however, large-scale dam construction is under way in Nibutani. A large portion of the land is owned by Ainu as a result of the government's land redistribution plan under the Former Primitive People Protection Law.* Although the Ainu people once owned all the mountains, rivers, and ocean around Hokkaido, the mountains have become nationalized or corporate property, the rivers have been expropriated by

---

*The Hokkaido Former Primitive People Protection Law was enacted in 1901. While a certain area of land was distributed to Ainu through this law, many Ainu lost their land to pay their debts. Currently there is a movement to pass the New Ainu Law, which respects the rights of indigenous people.

the Ministry of Construction and Fishery Cooperatives, and what land was left is now being taken away. Facing this situation, two people of Ainu descent appealed to the Hokkaido Land Expropriation Committee: "We should at least have the right to catch salmon, the main staple of our diet."

It is not so long ago that the northern part of the Japanese archipelago, particularly from Hokkaido to Chishima, belonged to Ainu. Japanese neighbors [*wajin* in Japanese; *shisamu* in Ainu] advanced northward. The Shakushain War, which was the last major Ainu armed resistance against Japan, ended in a catastrophic defeat for the Ainu. Thereafter, forced labor, fraud, and plunder became routine; the land was encroached upon and taken away.

At the beginning of the Meiji period, all Ainu land was nationalized. Forests and mountains on which Ainu people had always lived were "legitimately" stolen in the name of "public forests" or "imperial estates." It became a crime for the Ainu to cut a tree or hunt a deer in the forest behind their houses. Even catching salmon became a crime.

Kayano Shigeru, one of the two Ainu who appeared before the expropriations committee, is the director of the Nibutani Ainu Cultural Resource Center. He describes his own experience:

> A policeman with a sabre came into the house and asked my father, "Ready to go, Seijiro?" My father prostrated himself on the wooden floor and answered, "Yes." I saw his tears drop on the floor, but I was too young to understand why. It was horrible after that. I heard that the salmon my father had caught to feed us until the day before was illegal. My father walked off with the policemen in the direction of Hiratori. I followed him crying, while other adults tried to take me back. I still remember the adults as well as my father telling me that, "Your father will be back soon," but only in tears.

The Ainu, who had lived by fishing and hunting, were deprived of all the rights of indigenous peoples, except for a plot of approximately 5 hectares per household, which was later distributed by the government under the Former Primitive Peoples Protection Law.

Construction on the Nibutani dam was launched eighteen years ago along with the inauguration of the Eastern Tomakomai Large-Scale Industrial Complex Development Plan. The water dammed up at Saru River was to flow into Mu River for use by the industrial complex. Unfortunately, after a period of rapid economic growth, Japanese industries did not reach this region, and the development plan was discouraged. However, the dam construction went ahead full steam even while its purpose changed to "multiple use," including flood control. Kayano asked the committee whether the area really needs this water supply for its industries.

In Nibutani, about thirty Ainu households had agricultural land for which they could be compensated, but none of them were willing to sell the land of their ancestors. Many of them, however, were in debt to the Agricultural Cooperative, because Japan's agriculture has suffered from economic decline. In 1984, the mayor of Hiratori and a departmental head of Muroran Development Construction reached a secret agreement on compensation for Ainu land, but without consulting the Ainu concerned. Under this agreement, independent Ainu farmers would be given an additional year's income for the land as a special fund so that they could restructure their lives.

Despite the questionable way in which the terms of compensation had been arrived at, the compensation proceeded according to the secret agreement. Kaizawa Tadashi, the vice-director of Hokkaido Utari Association, is the other Ainu landowner who attended the expropriation hearings. "In the past," he lamented, "we were cheated of our land for alcohol. Today, we are fooled by money, and we are losing the land for a pittance. To compensate for our long history of oppression, we could claim reimbursement for lost income of the last eighty years."

In any case, all the Ainu descendants except for Kaizawa and Kayano were persuaded and approved the land expropriation, while legal procedures took place as scheduled by the government. For example, the notification on the submission of grievances was posted on the public bulletin board with other documents, but Kaizawa and Kayano did not know about it until their friend told them a few days before the deadline. They submitted the letter of grievance to the governor of Hokkaido on time, albeit without any response, and they received an order to leave the land one and a half years later.

Given these incidents, the committee held a hearing in Sapporo on February 15, 1988, accompanied by the two Ainu claimants. All the testimony was officially recorded. Kayano and Kaizawa described the suffering of the Ainu nation for several hundred years and made final appeals. Kaizawa stressed that the forests next to Cotan (the Ainu village where he lives) are currently owned by a cooperative and should be returned to the Ainu. Kayano focused on redeeming the right to catch salmon.

The case of the salmon is particularly problematic. Although the Nibutani dam will have salmon runs, the *yana* (a device to chase fish into a net) set at the mouth of the river by the Togawa Fishery Cooperative prevents salmon from swimming upstream. Kayano has visited Canada, Alaska, and Sweden and observed that the right of indigenous peoples to fish or hunt for their own consumption is protected. Kayano hopes that the traditional Ainu method of salmon fishing will contribute toward sustaining traditional Ainu culture. It has been over eight months since the two Ainu made their final appeal. An additional petition signed by more than one hundred residents of Nibutani has been submitted as well. Dam construction is proceeding, however, while no response has come from the committee. The indirect pressure from the contractor is on the rise. The local authority of Hiratori simply expresses their dilemma on who has a right to salmon fishing. Monbetsu Fishery Cooperative was not willing to comment because they have not heard anything officially.

1988

The Appeal of the Ainu People: An Open Letter to the Prime Minister

Dear Prime Minister Takeshita Noboru:

I realize that you must be busy with the Recruit scandal, the consumption tax, and free trade issues, but I would like to ask you to consider an important problem. Hence, I write from Australia.

Today, a ceremony took place between a Japanese construction company, Kumadani-gumi, and representatives of various aboriginal groups. People danced and performed various rituals to celebrate the signing of a contract. This ceremony was done to celebrate Kumadani-gumi's cooperative venture with Australian corporations to search for gold. In this process, Kumadani-gumi attempted to win the consent of the aboriginal people because the gold prospecting impinged on aboriginal land.

As the Japanese "aborigines"—the Ainu people—maintain, Hokkaido was neither sold nor lent to the Japanese; instead the Japanese one-sidedly invaded and stole the land from the Ainu people through force. There is no way to argue this fact. The same is true in the case of Australia. The Australian aborigines did not sell or lend their land to the English and other Europeans; the latter simply invaded and conquered. In the case of Australia, for example, the aborigines of Tasmania numbered several thousand, but they had all died a century after their contact with the European "white devil."

However, there is one difference between the fate of two aboriginal peoples. The difference is symbolized by the ceremony today.

Although there are differences between states in Australia, the government of the Northern Territories recognizes aboriginal land rights. Of course, the land is a desert or semidesert that the aborigines were forced to settle after the European invasion, but later political struggles ensured land rights.

In the case of the Ainu people, after all the land of Hokkaido was taken away from them, only some land and forest have become "public" (in effect, partially returned to the Ainu people). In this regard, the difference is enormous: the Australian situation is so much more democratic.

If the ostensibly useless land in the Australian Northern Territories turns out to possess gold or uranium, it is not possible for corporations to enter without the consent of the indigenous people. Of course, there are problems with this arrangement, but in principle it seems to be respected. This has been achieved through the struggles of the aboriginal people and some progressive white people.

Kumadani-gumi and their Australian allies negotiated with the aborigines for over a year to win the right to search for minerals. While over two hundred companies requested it, only six have been successful. The focus of the negotiation was the amount of profit that would be repatriated to the aboriginal people.

To be sure, Australia is a white-dominated society, but the savagery of Japan is striking in comparison to the Australian policy toward the aborigines. Is there any country that respects the rights of indigenous people less than Japan?

Prime Minister Takeshita, at least Japan can meet world standards of decency and not embarrass ourselves. This is something that you can do. It relates to your favorite concerns—like "home-town" and "the environmental problem."

1989

The "Export" of Women
from the Philippines

Members of the Bolshoi Ballet and strippers both dance; hence, both are entertainers. There are many agencies and brokers in Japan that promote foreign artists or entertainers. If serious artists who perform classical or folk arts stand on the bright side of this industry, entertainers at night clubs, hotels, and restaurants occupy the darker side, while performers in "special shows" at inns, strip theaters, and cheap bars are in the darkest part of all.

Before Japan's rapid economic growth, Japanese women occupied the dark spheres. Recently, however, a change has occurred in this industry; foreign women constitute a large portion of those working in the darkest sector.

Some time ago Japanese girls from poor farming families went (or were forced to go) to port cities in Southeast Asia; they were called *karayukisan*. Today we are seeing a reverse flow of girls—and boys—who are coming from Southeast Asia to Japan for money. The largest portion of them come from the Philippines. They are called *gyaku-karayukisan* or

nihonyukisan.* They are professional or semiprofessional entertainers, barmaids, gay boys, and strippers. How were they
brought to Japan? Evidently, they are recruited by talent
import promoters, or "performer promoters," or *yobiya* [bro-
kers]. I happened to become acquainted with a fifty-year-old
director of a medium-sized promotion agency. I asked him—
I will call him Kumazawa—to take me along on one of his
recruiting trips to the Philippines. Through the eyes of this
agent, I wanted to investigate the activities and "logic" of these
promoters as part of the Japanese economy.

Kumazawa went to the Philippines for the first time four
years ago [in 1977]. Since then, he has made nearly fifty round
trips to the country to spend a week or ten days per month.
He said that traveling to the Philippines is not much different
from traveling within Japan. It was true, indeed. Here is an
example. The attendants on the Thai air line distributed a
disembarkation card and a customs declaration form to be
filled out in English. Kumazawa ignored the paper, left them
on the plane, and went out to Manila Airport, where heavy
rain had just ended. He wore overshoes and jeans, which he
knows to be the most suitable clothing for the rainy season.
At Customs and Immigration Control, Kumazawa stub-
bornly insisted to the officials that he did not understand
English. He might have been resisting the tendency to assume

---

*Karayukisan means, literally, "people going to China."
Gyaku-karayukisan means "reverse *karayukisan*," and *nihonyukisan*
means "people going to Japan." By the mid-1980s, the common term for
Filipina and other Asian women who came to work in the "water trade"
(the encompassing Japanese term for women entertaining men in some
capacity) was *Japayukisan,* the same meaning as *nihonyukisan.*

that English, a language spoken in only part of the world, is regarded as the international language for no good reason. Even if one does not understand English, the person still has a right to travel in the world, and therefore responding to officials' questions in English should not be required. The customs official gave up on Kumazawa and stamped his passport after examining his bag.

Kumazawa, with moustache and dark glasses, went out of the airport and found a young man of about thirty waiting for him in a car. His name was Kultsu; in Manila he serves as Kumazawa's translator, secretary, driver, and mediator.

Kultsu brought us to a middle-class hotel, or more correctly, a kind of rental apartment, located close to downtown Manila. This type of apartment is more convenient than a hotel for interviewing women entertainers and their managers and testing their performance because nobody checks the visitors. The kitchen attached to the room is also useful. Kumazawa likes to feed visitors who come around meal-time, but it would be too costly to take all of them to a restaurant. With the kitchen, he gets some young entertainers who know him to cook for him.

On the day he arrived, Kumazawa went to an agency that sends entertainers from the Philippines to Japan and arranged for auditions the next day. Kumazawa also paid the agency with Japanese currency.

When he returned to the apartment, four entertainers were waiting for him; they had heard that Kumazawa had arrived in Manila. All four of them had been to Japan through Kumazawa and his agency. They came to see him because they wanted to go back to Japan or because they wanted to introduce their friends, who were interested in going to Japan.

Kumazawa's business started as soon as he arrived, and continued for ten days from morning to midnight until the last minute of his stay in the Philippines. Because it was the rainy season, he did not leave Manila except for a day trip to Baguio, a resort area in Luzon. In the dry season, he often flies to other islands—Cebu or Mindanao—for business.

Kumazawa has three major tasks. First, he sees entertainers or managers who visit his apartment and evaluates their commodity value as entertainers. Second, he holds auditions at several places. Third, he goes to tourist restaurants, night-clubs, and beer gardens and recruits candidates from among the performers. He does the first two tasks during the day and the third at night.

Once Kumazawa assesses a candidate's marketability, he draws up a contract and initiates the procedure for her or his travel to Japan. He told me that one business trip to the Philippines usually generates twenty-five to fifty contracts. None of them are great artists. Most of them receive around $500 per month, which is lower than what most foreign entertainers are paid in Japan. While many are singers or dancers, there are some who are strippers. Entertainers with several abilities, however imperfect, are more desirable than those who have mastered only one art.

The audition on the first day was held at a cabaret that is open only at night. All the candidates were singers. They appeared on the stage alone or in groups of two to four and sang with a band. On the way back to the apartment after the audition, Kumazawa commented that none were pretty or good singers, and therefore they were unmarketable.

Around dusk, we went to the only nude teahouse in Manila. This teahouse is owned by the son of the mayor of Manila;

hence, no other place in Manila has permission to provide service with all-nude dancers. More than ten nude dancers performed, one after another. Their dancing was explicitly sexual—using their *hoto* to pick up a bill that a customer put on top of a beer bottle, or raising a leg at customers' tables to show their *hoto*, and so on.* About half of the dancers in the teahouse had worked in Japan and have known Kumazawa for a long time. One dancer asked Kumazawa in Japanese to give her another chance to go to Japan, while others introduced their friends to Kumazawa as candidates.

We had dinner at a tourist restaurant surrounded by souvenir shops. A dancer in an Arabian-style costume appeared on the stage after a series of acrobats, magicians, and dancers. Kumazawa told me that he had already made a contract with her during his previous stay in Manila; she was to come to Japan within the year.

Such is an ordinary day in Manila for Kumazawa. In the morning, visitors, candidates, managers or entertainers who want to introduce friends wake Kumazawa up. Dancers change into their bikinis in the bathroom and perform their best dance in the bedroom to rock or popular music from Kumazawa's small cassette recorder. Kumazawa examines these candidates very carefully. For example, he observes the body line to see whether a dancer has had a child or not. He checks their physical condition to evaluate their value as a commodity. These commodities are bought on actual or anticipated demand in the Japanese market. More concretely, he either looks for specific types of entertainers to fill orders

---

* Hoto is the ancient Japanese word for vagina.

from cabarets, hotels, bars, clubs, and spas in Japan or finds promising entertainers, signs them up for his production company, and places them on the market in Japan.

After his examination, Kumazawa takes pictures of promising entertainers and adds their names to the list of candidates, while he ignores those who are not valuable. If a candidate is very promising, he immediately draws up a contract. About half of the managers are middle-aged women. Many were entertainers themselves. Among all the auditions I observed, gay dancers were the most zealous.

Who are these women? To answer this question, we should look at the pool from which these candidates are drawn: the nightlife scene in Manila. There are many women hanging around beer gardens—perhaps ten times as many women as customers at bars on one street. The women with the lowest status are those who work for prostitution agencies, servicing sex tourists from Japan and other countries.

I visited one of those agencies with Kumazawa. The building looked like a tea-house and there were no customers on the first floor. When we went up to the second floor, however, I was stunned by what I saw: in a large amphitheater, seventy to eighty women were standing holding number plates. All of them were watching Kumazawa, Kultsu, and myself—the only males in the room. A third of them also winked at us. I felt extremely embarrassed, and I would have charged out of the room if I had not come there as a reporter. While trying to calm down, I asked Kumazawa and Kultsu whether I could take a picture. They became upset and stopped me. Having nothing else to do, I observed the women furtively; I found a pair of angry eyes among a bunch of winks, and sweet, bitter, cold smiles. I think I understood. She must be furious at the unjust class structure or the humiliation of her nation. She might have come here to support her impoverished family by throwing away her pride. Perhaps she might even be a spy from the New People's Army.* I started imagining that if I have any choice, I would interview the angry woman. At that moment, Kumazawa stood up and said, "Let's go." The crowd of women realized that we were leaving without choosing any of them. A stir of lament, dissatisfaction, or perhaps even anger ran through the room.

Besides these women at the bottom of the system, who are the women from whom entertainers are drawn? They are in fact ordinary people in the Philippines. They are neither from rich families nor from mountain tribes. They are not from families of dancers or actors either. In fact, there are few natives of Manila; many of the women are from provincial agricultural or fishing villages. Much like refugees to Saigon and Phnom Penh who rapidly raised the population of those cities, many Filipina women flow into the cities from families that cannot survive by farming or fishing. This is a consequence of the neocolonial economic structure. The women come to Manila from Cebu, Mindanao, and other smaller islands, and they constitute the reserve of entertainers who seek the Japanese market. These women often work in the gay quarter because it is the easiest and most profitable one for them in Manila.

---

*The New People's Army (NPA) is the militant group affiliated with the Philippine Communist Party (CPP). Since its establishment in 1969, the NPA has developed in Samar Island and in mountainous areas in northern Luzon Island. Its power was a serious threat to the Marcos government in the 1970s and 1980s.

In some cases, women are simply sold by deception. Two young women, for example, sought help from a Catholic nun on a boat from Cebu to Manila. The women told the nun that they were contracted as maids to work in Manila, and that their respective mothers received 100 pesos (about ¥3500 or $27) from an agent. As soon as they boarded the boat, however, they were forced to become prostitutes for Chinese merchants in first-class cabins. According to the nun, there were about twenty such women on the boat.

While many women migrate to Manila or other large cities, only a few lucky ones have the talent in singing and/or dancing to succeed in rudimentary, nonprofessional auditions. Among the lucky ones, a few can get contracts to work in Japan or other countries; the job may be low-paying by the host country's standards, but lucrative by Filipino standards.

As Kumazawa's business card shows, his agency has a work permit from the Philippines Ministry of Labor. Thus, he can legally import the women into Japan. In fact, the women Kumazawa brings to Japan obtain an entertainer visa (a specialized visa), which is perfectly legal, although some problems could arise at actual work sites.

Fewer than half, however, arrive in Japan through legal channels. Most women who work as waitresses or illegal prostitutes in Japan are issued tourist visas. Kumazawa says:

> I cannot imagine why average Filipinas from ordinary families would go to Japan simply for sightseeing. It is only possible for a handful of daughters from very rich families, who, however, would never travel alone. Therefore, all the women who come to Japan with tourist visas can be considered women of "that kind." Well, if they can enter Japan legally, nothing will go wrong unless the police catch them in the very act of a crime.

How do you import women of "that kind"? What follows is based on the statements of those involved in the business. Filipinas are imported to Japan by individual Japanese or through an agency. Managers of nightclubs or bars may visit the Philippines themselves and select women for their business; a Japanese male tourist may become intimate with a Filipina and take her back with him; a Filipina may be tricked into a fraudulent marriage and brought to Japan, and so on. Agencies that specialize in illegal deals often work in concert with travel agencies in the Philippines. In the Philippines, a Japanese term *yakuza* is commonly used. *Yakuza* originally meant "gangsters," but now it is widely used to refer to all bad Japanese people, particularly illegal traders and import-export dealers.

Certainly, real gangsters may be involved in the import of Filipinas. Here is an example. A Filipino travel agency mixed up with a Japanese broker charges a much higher fee for obtaining a passport for Filipina applicants. Sometimes the fee includes a bribe. If applicants do not have enough money, then the travel agency lets Japanese brokers make an advance. To obtain a tourist visa to enter Japan, Filipinas need ¥500,000 to ¥600,000 to show the Japanese consulate or immigration control. The Japanese broker lends the necessary amount of money to an applicant and gets it back after she enters Japan, often by withdrawing it from her earnings. To stay in Japan for a longer period, visitors require a reference who is unrelated to the hotel or club business. The broker takes care of this by paying a third party to stand security for the Filipinas. Basically, a paid guarantor simply has to state to immigration officials that Filipinas are relatives of somebody with whom she or he was well acquainted in the Philippines;

then everything should be fine. Even if the Filipina's illegal employment as a waitress, for example, is revealed, the guarantor will be excused by saying, "I did not know about it," while the Filipina will be sent home. Even if illegal brokers' names are exposed and placed on the blacklist, it does not prevent them from flying to the Philippines.

Thus the methods of export are various: simple or sophisticated, legal or illegal. The Filipinas who are imported by legal contract, as is the case with Kumazawa, are less vulnerable than those who are imported through gangster-brokers. These women may be forced to become prostitutes in Japan, as one twenty-three-year-old woman from Cebu Island found out. She worked as a barmaid upon her arrival in Japan. One night in the third week, a customer invited her to his house and she accepted. The man drove her somewhere far away, to a deserted place up in the mountains. She was confined to the house, watched by a gangster guard, and forced to be a "free" prostitute. Just before her visa expired, she was returned to the responsible broker, but the broker said nothing to the gang. According to her, she was sold off to a *yakuza* group. Threatened that she would be killed if she went to the police, the woman left Japan and returned to Cebu, telling her friends in Manila never to go to Japan.

I have discussed how Filipinas are "produced" and "exported" to Japan. But why do most of the entertainers come from the Philippines, rather than from other poor countries in Southeast Asia? I believe that the answer lies in "internationalization," or more bluntly speaking, the completeness of the cultural colonization process in the Philippines. This is the only country in Asia that uses only English for traffic signs on freeways as well as on many other roads. (While India is also a multiethnic country, it takes robust cultural protection measures.) Most major newspapers in the Philippines are available only in English; those in native languages are all local, small-scale community papers. Television broadcasting is bilingual—in English and local languages—and contributes to the dissemination of contemporary U.S. songs directly to the Filipino population. Thanks to this internationalization, it is not difficult for the Philippines to become a supplier of semi-skilled technical labor.

Of course, such so-called internationalization is merely a kind of colonialism, irrelevant to native cultures in the Philippines. We cannot ridicule the Philippines for confusing these two concepts, as Japan also has many intellectuals who cannot distinguish between them.

A more essential factor behind labor export is the neocolonial economic structure. While the direct traders of this "commodity" are brokers, the producers of the commodity, according to the principles of market economy, are U.S. capital, particularly in the banana industry, and Japanese capital, particularly in the steel industry. For example, Kawasaki Steel took over a fishing village, and the residents were forced to move into prefabricated houses. They could not survive there and became refugees. Direct investment from U.S. and Japanese corporations enhances economic colonization. As a result, local industries are devastated, the economic gap between different regions widens, and more people become displaced. In this situation, if recruiters are not selective, there are many volunteers to go to Japan. The Filipino economic structure responds readily to Japanese demand. In this regard, petty effort cannot bring a solution to the problem of labor export.

The picture we see here is indeed like a model of contemporary capitalism and neocolonialism. Brokers merely play the role of small-scale contractors at the bottom of the whole structure. There are stories of bad experiences in Japan, like the one I described earlier, but they do not seem to contribute to the decline of *nihonyukisan*. The situation will change only when there is a dramatic transformation in the economic relations between Japan and the Philippines or in the political system of the Philippines.

There are some factors in the Philippines pushing for change. The corruption in the Marcos government has become comparable to that of the former South Vietnam, while the NPA's guerrilla warfare has intensified. Traditionalism as a reaction to overextended economic and cultural colonialism is making a comeback. These new movements, which have been relatively insignificant so far, may cause a major change some day. "Well, this business might be terminated suddenly. I should be prepared for that time," said Kumazawa on our return flight to Japan.

1981

III
The Culture of Conformity and the Impoverished Intellectuals

A Theory of Tadpole Society

When I was a child, thousands of tadpoles swam in groups in ponds and rice paddies. On close observation, one would realize that they did not swim in groups because of leadership or from individual will. If one of the group turned sideways, all of them turned sideways. The behavioral principle is to follow what the others are doing.

The Japanese behavioral principle is like that of tadpoles. Neither theory nor logic nor ethics underlies or informs Japanese behavior. Quite simply, a Japanese looks around and does what others are doing; that is the principle of action. Hence, Japanese have trouble with theory, logic, and ethics; they cannot argue or debate.

The tadpole society is a product of the Ministry of Education. It is, of course, easy to administer a society of tadpoles. In order to create a tadpole society, the Ministry of Education defines education as regurgitation. The Ministry of Education decides what is good to think, while denigrating individual opinion. Individuality is punished, and no one is encouraged to think on one's own. And things are getting worse.

Perhaps a tadpole society was functional for a village community of the past. But in larger, complex societies, especially in international affairs, it doesn't work very well.

It is often said that the Japanese are unique. Some say that the Japanese love nature. But is this really true? Isn't the reverse the case? Some say that our language is unique. A famous critic, Shimizu Ikutarô,* once wrote that while European sentences start with the subject and end with the predicate [following the pattern S-V-P, or subject-verb-predicate], the verb comes at the end in Japanese. However, a similar syntax exists in Ainu, Korean, and Basque. There is nothing special about Japanese grammar; it is simply that the critic is ignorant. In theories of Japanese uniqueness, these mistakes abound.

However, I do think that the Japanese pattern—what I call the tadpole society—is unique. Recently, the problem of *ijime* —students bullying other students—has become serious in elementary and junior high schools. The root of *ijime* is that some students are harassed and beaten up for being different from the majority. There is nothing intrinsic in the source of bullying—rather, anyone who is different becomes the target.

When I write on the Nanjing massacre, the right wing criticizes me and some call me a traitor. However, who is the patriot and who is the traitor? Because Japan is a tadpole society, the world is beginning to hate Japan. I would like to change this. For example, because Germany attempts to bear

---

*Shimizu was an influential progressive sociologist and intellectual. However, he gradually turned toward the right and by the 1980s became a reactionary nationalist.

the burden of its war responsibility, Germany has some credibility among neighboring countries. In Japan, because there has been no such effort, we are still not trusted by our neighboring Asian countries. I am patriotic because I want Japan to be respected in the international community.

1991

Foreign Embassies in Japan

What happens when you call the Swedish embassy in Japan? As soon as the operator, a young Japanese woman, picks up the telephone, she says "Swedish embassy" in English. The point is, personnel at the Swedish embassy in *Japan*, which is located in *Japan*, speak *English* to a Japanese person. This is not true everywhere. Take for instance, the People's Republic of China. Let us call the Chinese embassy located in Ebisu, Tokyo. The operator will answer in Japanese without fail. How about the embassy of the Federal Republic of Germany? They answer in German. My research showed the following: France, Holland, the United Arab Emirates, Italy, and South Vietnam all answered in Japanese; the United Kingdom, the United States, Indonesia, Australia, and Pakistan answered in English; the Republic of Korea answered in Korean. Foreign embassies choose either English, their own language, or Japanese to communicate with the Japanese public.

What I am trying to point out should be obvious to you by now. For foreign embassies located in Japan, using Japanese to communicate with the Japanese public should be a natural rule, not only as a common-sense gesture of diplomatic etiquette but for the sake of pragmatism as well. Isn't the primary mission of a foreign embassy in Japan the building of fraternity between its particular country and the Japanese people? Those embassies that use English to the Japanese public are expressing, first, their arrogance that they are not there to deal with the Japanese people (or at least, not ordinary Japanese citizens); second, their collaboration with the hegemonic force of cultural and linguistic imperialism which turns English into the "universal language"; and finally, their lack of pride in their own language.

The embassies that use their own language are better than those that use English. However, using one's own language seems arrogant if it is a large and powerful country, while it seems somewhat pitiful if done by a small nation. All in all, as far as the use of language goes, it would be best for foreign delegations in Japan to use Japanese.

What about Japanese embassies in other countries? As far as I know, in "powerful" countries such as the United States or France, Japanese embassies use the language of the host country. But do they respond with Arabic in Saudi Arabia or Kuwait? Do they answer with Thai in Thailand or Vietnamese in Hanoi? Although I have not confirmed every case, the answer is most likely no. However, they probably do not use Japanese either. They are most likely to use the worst method, which is to respond with English in non-English-speaking countries, just like the Swedish embassy in Japan. Those who are responsible should reconsider the current policy.

1973

Why Can't We Squat?

In contemporary Japanese cities, we don't see people squatting. For myself, I only squat when I am in traditional Japanese bathrooms. Although I don't remember it very well, I must have squatted quite often when I was in elementary and secondary school. In my native village, adults still squat. When did I stop squatting?

The first time I found squatting strange was when I came to live in a city after graduating from high school. During school vacation, I was on my way back to my hometown. As I was waiting for my train, I noticed some four or five men in their forties who were all squatting; they were all people I knew. Why did these people, who squat every day, seem so strange?

I think the main reason is that they were wearing coats and ties. They were on their way somewhere and were wearing something they would never wear in their everyday life. They didn't fit very well—they looked awkward, farcical, and pathetic. The same was true when my father wore suits. When he was awkwardly wearing ill-fitting Western shoes on feet used to *geta* [clogs] and *zôri* [thongs], everyone could tell that he was a country bumpkin, although he never realized it.

When the besuited men all squatted together, they were an unbearable sight. European clothes don't look good when the wearer squats; they are not made for that culture. However, when these same men squat in farm clothes, they look fine. In fact, they look particularly appropriate—part of the pastoral scene. In contrast, if an English gentleman were to squat in rice paddies, that would just be hysterical.

In fact, in most non-European cultures, people squat rather naturally. This is certainly true among the people I've visited. In Saudi Arabia, squatting in the long robe is unproblematic and natural. The same is true in India or Pakistan. The Vietnamese also squat often. The naked men of the New Guinea highlands also squat; they look dignified.

However, from the moment one is clad in a suit this natural posture looks pathetic. An Arab, Indian, Pakistan, Vietnamese, or New Guinea highlander will also look like the Japanese men at the railway station.

The situation is not restricted to suits. When I visited a liberated zone in the Mekong Delta, a soldier told me: "In rural life, it was traditional for women to wear loose pants. However, recently, some women wear tight pants because of American influence. In Vietnam, when we sit outside, it is traditional to squat. In loose pants, this posture is unproblematic, but when women in tight pants do it, it is all rather embarrassing." When I told him that the same is the case for Japanese women in skirts, he started laughing.

Clearly, the problem is not squatting. Rather, the problem lies in wearing suits and squatting. The reason I was sensitive to the men from my hometown is because I had become part of the urban "suits culture." If I had continued to live in my hometown, I would not have found it out of the ordinary.

Squatting is a purely physical activity. In itself, it is not problematic. However, whether it is fitting or not depends on what one wears. Let's consider the background.

When I covered the Vietnam war, I had a chance to observe the posture of many American soldiers. Vietnamese translators or cameramen often squat. In contrast, American soldiers never squatted—or only when they absolutely had to. Obviously, they could squat if they had to. But in their culture, squatting is an odd and embarrassing posture.

Why don't American women wear the loose, baggy pants that Vietnamese women wear? Why doesn't an American man wear traditional Japanese attire? Why doesn't a Frenchman wear Arabic clothing? Of course, there are always exceptions. But my point concerns daily life. This can't be explained by utility. Coats and ties were born in the European climate and culture. They are particularly inappropriate for humid Japan, yet they have become the standard urban clothing.

I think it is clear that the power relations between the dominant and the dominated extend even to matters of clothing. At first, Europeans and the colonized looked at each other's clothing as, at worst, something exotic. However, as the power relations became established—as economic and military domination advanced—every aspect of the dominant culture became superior, including culture, habit, and language, but also skin color, facial structure, even body hair. The dominant believed in their superiority, the dominated were forced to think that way. In short a colonial relationship—enslavement—was established. This is not restricted to the relationship between Western and non-Western cultures. It is the same everywhere economic and military domination and invasion occur. This was the case for the relationship between Japan and Korea, or between Shamo [*wajin*, or ethnic Japanese] and Ainu. Most Shamo do not appreciate the great oral tradition of Ainu literature; the former think of themselves as superior even if unconsciously—to the latter.

Squatting is not in and of itself odd or ill-fitting. What is odd and ill-fitting is, rather, to wear coats and ties in a humid Japanese climate—an expression of the colonized, enslaved mentality.

One author recalls an experience when he was scolded by an American soldier. "When I squatted because I was drunk, a GI came up and yelled at me to stand up. In my drunken stupor, I remember thinking that Americans must find squatting unbearable." What a foolish and arrogant American soldier. As part of the invader culture, the ignorant and savage soldier thought himself superior to other peoples. If a GI were to yell at me, I would yell back: "Don't stand like a fool! Why don't you squat!"

1973

How to Dress at a Restaurant

Last summer, I went with a friend to a restaurant in a large Tokyo hotel. The evening view overlooking the Imperial Palace was especially beautiful. However, we could not enter the restaurant because we were not dressed appropriately. It was unfortunate, but nothing could be done.

I suppose that in countries like England and France, to which we aspire in our modernization efforts, dress codes are if anything more strict. I asked: "Then what should we wear?" The reply: "At least a coat. However, women can wear anything." "What if we wore traditional Japanese clothing?" The man at the counter paused and then answered: "No, you must wear Western clothes." "What if some Arab came in wearing Arabic clothing?" He paused again and said maliciously: "Well, it depends on the situation but I cannot decide, so perhaps you should ask the manager."

We can see the "colonized" spirit of Japanese hotels. They do not recognize traditional Japanese clothing—what we wear to weddings—as appropriate. If I wore traditional clothes, whether Japanese or Arab, to a first-rate hotel in Paris or London, I would assume that it would be appropriate.

I once went to a hotel in Hanoi that had been constructed during the French colonial period. I felt as though I had come to the Paris of the Bourbon monarchy. However, in the main restaurant of that hotel, the waitresses didn't speak any language other than Vietnamese. They were very kind and friendly, but they didn't find it necessary to know other languages. In contrast, at a first-class restaurant in Saigon (then South Vietnam), there are many waitresses and waiters who speak French or English. When I try to speak in Vietnamese, they look at me scornfully as someone who can't speak French or English. This is the spirit of the colonized; I am afraid that the Japanese are becoming like that.

1969

The Tamed Japanese:
The Achievement
of the Ministry of Education

In the past forty years, the Ministry of Education, controlled by the dominant Liberal Democratic Party, has promoted an educational policy that is destroying Japan. The consequences of the ministry's deleterious policy can be seen in the results of the National Achievement Test for junior high school students, which was published in 1985 for the first time in seventeen years.

In the report, the Ministry of Education notes that the intellectual attainment of junior high school students has improved and that schools have achieved their goal "quite well." In short, the ministry is pleased with the result of the National Achievement Test.

It seems to me, however, that the ministry's evaluation of the educational achievement is very much like that of parents who rejoice because their children mimic them and reproduce themselves in the same mold. In general, most people expect the next generation to learn from and praise what the earlier generation has achieved. The similar desire to reproduce the status quo motivates the Ministry of Education and its attitude toward educational achievement.

Here is an example of the kind of intelligence that bureaucrats in the Ministry of Education savor. According to Sada Tomoko of *Asahi Shinbun,* while nearly 90 percent of the students know the number of legs and the morphology of an insect, less than half of the students can correctly identify various features of the insect from an illustration. Further, fewer students can draw a picture of the insect. The report also says that students are incompetent in logical and creative thinking—in the ability to reason from observed data.

These results show that there is virtually no improvement in the intellectual level of students. The achievement of postwar education should be evaluated in the worst possible way. For the bureaucrats in the Ministry of Education, however, this outcome is worthy of high praise. This is simply because students are reproducing the mode of knowledge and thinking mastered by elite bureaucrats. In other words, the current educational policy is beneficial to those who would like to reproduce in the future the same social consciousness that reigns today. This perspective on education is, however, questionable to those, including myself, who would like to see children learning to grow as good human beings, not as good bureaucrats.

Incidentally, I must emphasize that it is not necessarily the public schools that blindly follow the policy of the Ministry of Education. Some reputable private schools are far more submissive in reproducing future bureaucrats.

The Japanese "intelligence," judging from the results of the achievement tests, stresses memorization skills. Memorizing all the information in dictionaries and encyclopedias may be valuable in certain instances. The memory capacity of a human being is, however, much more limited than a simple computer. What is more important than memorizing existing knowledge is being able to use knowledge as an instrument to develop something new. The bureaucrats in the Ministry of Education obviously do not understand this point and regard the ability to memorize as a major indicator of intelligence.

According to the report, urban children demonstrated their "intelligence" much better than their counterparts in rural areas. This result is not surprising, for the criterion of intelligence is the ability to memorize. Rural children can identify insects or other creatures much better than urban children, but they cannot get a good grade because of their lack of memorized knowledge. Urban children, on the other hand, have memorized the number of legs an insect has and thus attain better marks on the "intelligence" test, although many of them cannot identify the insect when they see it with their own eyes.

The 1985 White Paper on the Development of Science and Technology lists three factors essential for creative discoveries and inventions, based on the study of scientists and technical specialists who were awarded the Nobel Prize and/or the Japan Academy Award: first, childhood experience with natural phenomena; second, the development of curiosity about natural phenomena; and, finally, an ardent desire to pursue learning.

The Japanese system of education, which aims to reproduce bureaucrats, destroys creativity and true intelligence. In fact, these negative tendencies can be observed even more intensely in the recent survey of junior high school students. They are the future leaders of Japan. Thus, the educational policy of the Ministry of Education is, as I mentioned earlier, ruining the Japanese.

What supports such an educational policy that perpetuates the fallacious type of "intelligence" is the Japanese behavioral principle of following what others are doing and avoiding doing something different. A reporter from National Public Radio in Washington, D.C., described Japanese behavior in the following way: once a problem is solved, the Japanese immediately start running in the same direction.

In general, Japanese behavior is based on the principle of emulating the majority. This is one of the causes of the Japanese soldiers' atrocious behavior during the World War II. When other soldiers were engaged in a massacre, no individual would dare to stop it. On the contrary, everybody simply participated in the inhumane act.

Some time in the future, I would like to write a book entitled *What You Should Not Learn from Japan* and have it translated into foreign languages so that people outside of Japan can know more about Japanese educational and behavioral deficiencies. I may be exposing a shameful aspect of our society, but I will do so as a patriot.

1986

The Destruction
of Elementary Education

A public elementary school in Tokyo has a rule that students must go to school in a group to prevent traffic accidents. Accordingly, five to fifteen children living in a neighborhood meet on the street in the morning and walk to school together. Usually the oldest student becomes the leader of the group.

In a neighborhood where one of my friends lives, there is one such group of six students. A boy, P, is the only sixth-grade student in the group and the others are all in lower grades. P, however, does not participate in this group walk because his mother will not let him. But her rationale has nothing to do with the somewhat common critique that this group practice enhances the right-wing ideology. No, she refuses to allow her son to join the group walk to school because P cannot promise an adequate commitment to the group. Since P is preparing for entrance exams, hoping to get into either a private junior high school or one that is attached to a national university, he studies until late at night to complete the homework assigned by his private tutor. In the morning, he arrives at school just in time or sometimes even late. Given this situation, a fourth-grade student was forced to lead the group instead of P.

P does not take his textbooks to school. While cleaning his room, his mother put them in a garbage can by mistake and a hired housekeeper burned them. P has made no effort to replace them, however. What he studies for entrance exams is far more advanced than the content of school textbooks, and he disdains them because they are "useless."

Among P's classmates, there are three other students who study for exams, pushed by extremely "education-conscious" mothers.* One of them once threw toilet rolls out of the bathroom window. When a teacher told him not to do so, he did the same thing again, only with toilet rolls he brought from home. This was not the typical behavior of a bad boy. He was releasing his frustration, which had been repressed by his education-conscious mother.

The children who study intensely for entrance exams are often arrogant and rash. They ridicule school and disrupt teachers who try to teach other students. Thus they are a real nuisance to other students. Their parents are, however, insensitive to such a reality. The parents' short-sighted selfishness is reflected in their children, who gradually become brats in class. These children are obviously the victims of their parents.

The brats will probably enter private schools or schools attached to national universities, advance to top universities,

---

*The Japanese term is *kyôiku mama*, literally, "education mother." In postwar Japan, *kyôiku mama* became a common character type among Japanese housewives.

and ultimately become cold and cruel élitists. We can only anticipate that the number of "brats" will gradually increase and eventually dominate Japanese society.

1979

Standardized Education

The inscription on a four-thousand-year-old tablet reads: "The youth of today are corrupt." Indeed, parents and older people have always complained about the behavior of youth. Paradoxically, it is evident that society has worked well despite the persistence of imperfect youth. Perhaps our concern with youth may be pointless; perhaps we should simply let youth do whatever they want and cease worrying about our nation's future.

Is such an attitude toward youth proper? Human history tells us that some nations actually disappeared. The Tasmanians have completely disappeared from the earth. The Aztecs have ceased to exist as a culture, while the Cham in central Vietnam were almost exterminated at one time and barely continue to exist. Countries that were invaded and colonized for a long time before gaining independence, including India, Korea, and Vietnam, have also experienced crises of survival.

Why do nations disappear? Why were some countries invaded and colonized? Internal factors may contribute to the fall of nations. Immediately before its disappearance or colonization, a nation is usually dysfunctional; its future was obviously not very bright.

Recently I investigated two incidents involving high school students; my report was published as *The Revenge of the Children*. Although I am not an expert on education, the seriousness of the problem shocked me. Japan is not sound, and I do not think that it will get better.

I would like to focus on one problem in education: one value system controls Japanese youth; they are brainwashed to think and judge everything based on one standard. Consequently, various symptoms have appeared among children. For example, an increasing number of children are indifferent; they do not find anything interesting or exciting. This is a natural consequence of growing up under the dominant influence of a single standard.

Suppose that the world is dominated by a single standard of musical proficiency. In Japan, a great composer like Mitsuzaki Kenkô would have the most political and economic power, and singers, even awful ones, would earn more money and lead a better life than lawyers, physicians, or bureaucrats. Senior or junior high school students would diligently study singing and composition to enter a good music school, and teachers would compete over the number of students who successfully enter music schools. Cram schools would concentrate on teaching piano or *shakuhachi*, singing, or music composition.* The "losers" who could not pass the entrance

---

* "Cram schools" [*juku*] meet after school or on weekends to prepare students for entrance examinations, usually to college, but even for junior high schools. *Shakuhachi* is a traditional Japanese musical instrument.

exams for music school would become teachers, bureaucrats, physicians, factory workers, journalists, painters, and novelists. The people who are not musicians would be considered less worthy and suffer a severe inferiority complex.

Japan today faces a similar situation. Diversity in human capability is undermined, and excessive stress is placed on one ability: memorization. Children "study" by memorizing from the first day at elementary school. Even incompetent students with good "study" skills advance to first-class universities, while children with real talent may be repressed, lose interest, and eventually become apathetic. Thus the "brilliant" ones—many competent only in doing well on exams—become top bureaucrats and obtain well-paying jobs, grabbing millions of yen through abuse of public money and earning multiple pensions.*

The root of our educational problem clearly lies with adults who tolerate the current crisis. The problem of children is in fact the problem of our social structure.

1979

---

*Honda refers to the practice of *amakudari*, in which government bureaucrats after retirement land well-paying executive positions in the private sector.

Why Do Novelists Become Corrupt?

No one is born a reactionary. There are, however, people who are destined to be reactionary, such as princes and princesses. But even they can reform themselves if they actually start to work for a living like other people, and they may even end up becoming ashamed of their early life—they may become anti-reactionary. As has already been demonstrated in the case of the Emperor of Manchuria, Pu Yi,* if someone is educated about his own crime, he can atone for his sin and produce a memoir reflecting on his criminal past.

At present, however, to expect such a thing to happen to the Japanese would be an empty dream. The financiers, the LDP administration as their political representative, the police and the Self-Defense Forces as their repressive force, the Imperial Household Agency as their direct watchman, and the mass media as their defender and manipulator of *vox*

---

*The last emperor of the Qing Dynasty, memorably depicted in Bertolucci's film *The Last Emperor.*

populi—all are fully committed to preventing the Japanese people from reflecting on their history and reeducating themselves.

It is also rare for a novelist to start out her or his career as a reactionary. Although convinced right-wing writers, such as Mishima Yukio, are few, novelists such as Kaidaka Ken, who is currently well known only for his writing on fishing, used to be very seriously engaged in antifascist activities and peace movements. Even Ishihara Shintarô, who long ago became reactionary, once showed plenty of potential; contrary to his present political stance, Ishihara was a progressive figure back in 1960 during the Anpo struggle.*

The best example, however, is Ishikawa Tatsuzô, who was one of the most socially conscious novelists in Japan. Judging from his recent activities, it appears that he has abandoned the critical attitude and political courage of his youth. Keeping in mind people like Kawabata Yasunari, who drove himself to suicide as a result of complete self-degradation, I think that Ishikawa should be wary of getting trapped in the same path.

And Etô Jun was a progressive literary critic who, as we all know, transformed himself into a defender of the Emperor and imperial causes. Like Etô, Kobayashi Hideo is also a very sophisticated literary critic. When he backed Ishihara's can-

---

*The Anpo struggle refers to the opposition movement to the 1960 revision of the U.S.-Japan security treaty. This was perhaps the single largest political struggle in postwar Japanese history. Although the security treaty was forcefully renewed, it led to the downfall of the Kishi regime. See George Packard III, *Protest in Tokyo* (Princeton: Princeton University Press, 1966).

didacy for mayor of Tokyo, he did not engage in the scandalous and disgraceful behavior displayed by Kawabata when he backed a former chief of police, Hatano Akira, as a candidate for mayor of Tokyo. Despite those differences, however, Kobayashi and Kawabata are essentially of the same stripe.

At any rate, with a few exceptions, the majority of novelists are reactionary. However, many of them were not reactionary at first. Why do novelists turn to the right one after another? Why are most "popular" novelists reactionary?

To put it simply, novelists are part of a system that makes their rightward drift almost inevitable, just as a prince would surely become reactionary. Suppose an obscure young novelist succeeds in producing a superb work through diligent effort and becomes quite popular. Unlike in feudal times, writing is now big business. Therefore, if a writer produces a bestseller, then she or he can make millions of dollars, and the publisher will profit many times more. For publishers, a capable writer may be a goose that lays golden eggs. For this reason, publishers need to take care of the goose.

How do large publishers monopolize the breeding of their geese? The most effective method is to hang on to young writers after they have proved their ability. Of course, publishers do not just hand over cash to writers unconditionally. It is necessary to find a suitable justification. For instance, suppose a novelist decides to build a house, which requires ¥20 million. Our novelist asks his publisher for an advance on his royalties. If we suppose that the first edition of his novel sold 30,000 copies, his royalties would be ¥3 million [$23,400], which is sufficient for a down payment. Our novelist can take care of the rest with additional bank loans and so on. However, our novelist's publisher may ask him: "All together, how much would the house cost—¥20 million? Then, please allow us to pay all of it at once and take it as an advance on your future publications. In exchange, consider publishing all your future works with us."

The above example would be an extreme case, but it is certainly a well-used strategy among large publishers. A more common tactic is for publishers to entertain novelists by frequently taking them to bars and cabarets and surrounding them with attractive hostesses.* Another common practice used by publishers is to literally lock up novelists in hotel rooms and make them concentrate on writing in order to get them to produce their works faster. Of course, publishers pay all the expenses. There are novelists who live in hotels most of the time. In these ways, novelists' relations and obligations to their publishers become more complex and inescapable.

Another method is to reward novelists by "giving" them literary awards. Most major literary awards—the Akutagawa Award, the Tanizaki Award, the Noma Award, the Naoki Award and so on—are given by major publishers. This is precisely the problem. Critics are supposed to evaluate works in an "impartial" manner. However, the very publishers who give out the major awards also select the members of the award committees. The committee members often act as the puppets of major publishers. By using these literary awards as bait, major publishers lure novelists like fish, and as a result,

---

*Obviously, there are many well-known female writers in Japan. However, it is also the case that the world of publishing is male-dominated.

novelists begin to write for the literary journals published by the same publishers who presented them with awards.

In addition, major publishers employ talented editors. Writers develop personal relationships with their favorite editors. A writer would be hard-pressed to turn down working with an editor who reads works carefully, provides appropriate advice, is thoughtful and pleasant. It is not uncommon for writers to accept projects requested by publishers they dislike if these requests are made personally by their favorite editors. Even though writers may accept projects because of their favorite editors, all the profit is absorbed by the publishers, and as a result the writers end up contributing to the burgeoning publishing profits.

In this structure, it is common for "progressive" novelists to have their works published through reactionary publishers. Members of the so-called intelligentsia are usually astute as to whether a particular topic will be profitable or unprofitable for themselves. Therefore, it is very easy indeed for publishers to subliminally persuade the sensitive but idle intelligentsia to write novels targeted at winning awards. In this manner, "celebrities" are born as puppets of reactionary publishers. In most cases, puppets end up life as puppets.

To be sure, there are cases in which a novelist revolts against her or his reactionary publisher and begins to write materials considered "politically undesirable." Such writers become isolated from influential literary circles. They must rely solely on the support and solidarity of their readers. In order to be immune from the harassment and persecution of the establishment, such writers must either arm themselves theoretically or earn their living by some means other than writing. The majority of novelists lack both remedies and therefore have no choice but to be puppets. A similar structure can be found in the other arts as well.

Normal human beings live with dignity as long as they work and are rewarded in return. In a society that discriminates against honest labor, some workers do become servile. However, their servility is only superficial, and in most cases, if they are provoked, they become defiant. On the other hand, people who are overpaid are often truly servile. As they are overpaid, they begin to lose their dignity. For instance, try staging a debate between an overpaid celebrity novelist (or better yet, a capitalist) and a person who actually works hard for a living (a carpenter, an industrial worker, a farmer, and so on.) It would become obvious right away who has more dignity as a human being.

Also, the degree of social isolation tends to increase proportionally as an individual acquires greater material wealth. That is a natural consequence because rich people are in a constant fear of losing the money they have accumulated. In addition to protecting themselves from burglars and thieves, the rich may well become suspicious of their own relatives and even their own children; they inevitably end up being able to trust no one but themselves.

A similar situation prevails for novelists. In the current framework, attempts by novelists to exercise control over their work become futile for the same reason that only a dog can wag its own tail and not the other way around. Progressive novelists might present ideas for good projects to their publishers, but what normally happens is that their publishers politely and indirectly turn them down, saying, "We will carefully consider your suggestion." A goose is allowed to lay golden eggs and nothing else.

What can a novelist do? At this point, the only exit for the goose is to completely break its tie with its keeper and take some decisive measures. A novelist can either choose to write for small but democratic publishers or go into self-publishing. Inevitably, either choice will result in economic decline and self-sacrifice. To the goose that has become used to the luxurious and comfortable lifestyle provided by its keeper, it will be difficult and painful to return to life in the wild.

Young novelists may well be troubled by this contradiction. First of all, I do not think it is a good idea for writers to make their living solely by the act of writing itself. If writing is the sole source of income, the writer can be easily corrupted or broken down if threatened with having this arena taken away. Faced with this contradiction (many are never troubled at all!), most choose to eliminate the problem by becoming reactionary.

When novelists become reactionary, then there is no contradiction between what they believe and what they do. They will be puppets of their reactionary publishers, and this ultimately represents the interests of the reactionary regime. They will surely enjoy comfortable lives as long as the present capitalist system marches on. There will be job offers from major reactionary publishers and newspapers for these sold-out and complacent writers; they will be given high social status and fame, and there may even be openings for some (reactionary) political posts for them if they fancy such positions. Life will be sweet.

My aim was to highlight the existing structure, which makes it a rule rather than an exception for a novelist to become corrupt. Only a few novelists are able to maintain their political dignity in the long run. In general, it would be a mistake to expect too much from novelists, so we should appreciate as pleasant anomalies the small minority of novelists with exceptional dignity and talents when we encounter them.

1975

Who Is Responsible
for the Attempted Murder
of Mayor Motojima?

A pitifully shabby and malicious man made a cowardly attempt to assassinate Motojima Hitoshi, the mayor of Nagasaki, by shooting him in the back at point-blank range. Mayor Motojima fortunately survived, even though the bullet penetrated his chest. This whole fiasco was first triggered by the mayor's comment about the Emperor's war responsibility. The barbaric murder attempt serves to let the whole world know of the irrationality, the lack of ethics, and the premodern state of consciousness of the Japanese who have not changed at all since World War II.

It can be said that the assassin played an extremely unpatriotic role.* However, to a person such as a mayor, who must make public appearances, no matter how shabby or unpatri-

---

*Honda has repeatedly argued that the true patriots are those who would risk their lives to criticize the wrongdoing of their own country. In other words, a patriot in Honda's usage is exactly the kind of person whom the right wing calls "unpatriotic."

otic his opponents may be, they become a matter of grave concern when their behavior has such serious consequences, even death. Although this terrorist act was anticipated, the Nagasaki police force failed to protect the mayor, and it cannot escape responsibility. Why is it, then, that the resignation or demotion of the police chief and others in charge was not even discussed? To the public, inaction indicates that the police are soft on the right wing and possibly even indirectly collaborating.

Aren't conservatives in the city council who demanded elimination of the police guard because it was a "waste of tax money," and some right-wingers who are publicly applauding the "shabby and malicious" man, instigating and abetting murder? Needless to say, the fundamental character of any society or culture reveals itself in mundane and trifling phenomena. It is impossible that only the police were irresponsible and others were all decent and blameless.

Isn't our ineffectual mass media responsible? Mostly, they repeated clichés, such as "violence against freedom of speech cannot be tolerated."

Of course! Such a contention is an empty phrase. Do these journalists believe that such preaching would actually produce a positive effect? No. Because it is an empty phrase—because they have no influence whatsoever—they can reassuringly make such a claim. They will not make a meaningful and influential statement, because if they do, they know very well that terrorists would go after them. Or rather, journalists are afraid of the establishment that tolerates and even indirectly approves of terrorists. The people who exposed Mayor Motojima to terrorism are the people in the mass media, who are only keen on continuing unworthy and meaningless reporting.

Aren't our so-called progressive intellectuals, who were supposed to enlighten people, complicit? If the same arguments are articulated by many others, individuals such as Mayor Motojima who speak common sense would not be singled out as victims of terrorist attack.

What is it that is so radical or shocking in Mayor Motojima's statement? This is what he said:

> Judging from my experience in the Imperial Military and accounts by foreign and Japanese historians, I think the Emperor bears some responsibility for the war. However, as long as he was spared from the responsibility by the wishes of the majority of the Japanese people and the Allied forces and was made into the symbol of the new constitution, we must deal with the issues regarding the Emperor according to the aforementioned facts.

Just what is so radical about this statement? Motojima's statement clearly indicates that he accepts the existence and legitimacy of the Emperor. His war responsibility is a well-known and established fact. Even a right-wing ideologue like Akao Satoshi [the leader of Dai Nihon Aikokutô, or the Great Japan Patriotic Party] states: "If we said 'The Emperor bears no responsibility for the war,' we would be an object of ridicule for the rest of the world." Motojima made his sensationalized statement only because he was asked at the city council and he made the statement as an ordinary LDP-backed politician.

However, even this universally held knowledge is taken as "radical" in contemporary Japan, leaving Motojima isolated and prominent. Why? It is because the Japanese mass media and intellectuals dropped the issue of the Emperor's role in the war a long time ago. There has been no debate on the issue for quite some time. Except for underground magazines or political party newspapers, perhaps the only part of the mass media to still discuss the Emperor's war responsibility is this journal [*Asahi Jânaru*]. Despite his age, ninety-one-year-old Akao makes a sharp criticism of the mass media. "If they intend to pursue the war responsibility of the deceased Emperor, they should use their own words, instead of the words of the mayor of Nagasaki." Those pitiful journalists who are chanting the empty slogan of freedom of speech ought to realize that they are the ones who have voluntarily abandoned the very freedom that they preach about. They should also realize that the true cause of the assassination attempt on the mayor is their very silence on the Emperor's war responsibility. The majority of journalists, in a quite cowardly fashion, hid themselves behind the mayor's words, and kept themselves busy by reporting on subjects such as the Emperor's health condition (before his death) and his funeral.* Their attitude contributed to the shooting of the mayor.

And what about those who were once called "progressive intellectuals"? They have adjusted their public stance according to the political climate of our time, which has become much more reactionary since they made their debut in the early 1960s. This tendency is made clear just by comparing the path that they have taken in the last thirty years, intellectuals including Ishihara Shintarô, Etô Jun, Komatsu Sakyô,

---

*Indeed, in the few months before the Emperor's death, the Japanese mass media were awash with daily health reports of the octogenarian "symbol" of the country. For an insightful analysis, see Norma Field, *In the Realm of the Dying Emperor* (New York: Pantheon, 1991), chapter 3.

and others, who changed their position early on; Kaidaka Ken, who defected in between; and Oe Kenzaburô, Oshima Nagisa, and Nosaka Akiyuki, who became reactionary only recently.

The reason why I put quotation marks around "progressive intellectuals" is that they are not really intellectuals; they are pseudointellectuals. In the past I have repeatedly stated that courage and independence are important qualifications in an intellectual—qualities that these "intellectuals" obviously do not possess. Mayor Motojima reversed the path trod by the pseudojournalists and pseudointellectuals, who abandoned their freedom of speech.

Among the numerous critiques and reports of the assassination attempt on the mayor, one fact stands out: in the past, Motojima paid courtesy visits to a far-right political organization, Shokijuku, to which Motojima's sniper belongs. In short, Motojima was no more than a conservative mayor whose behavior was no different from the behavior of conservative local government heads all over Japan.

Based on this fact, we hear such criticism against Motojima as that of Oka Masaharu, minister of the Nagasaki Lutheran Church: "We cannot let the mayor become a hero.... Even though it may sound cruel, he was a sycophant of right-wingers who was attacked by a right-winger." Oka's criticism is misleading. Mayor Motojima and I have corresponded twice. In these letters, Motojima confessed in a remarkably humble fashion that he had been naive. The simple truth is that until he made his statement, Motojima had not changed his view on the Emperor's role in the war since 1945. He was only being honest with himself. He was surprised how the world around him changed after he made a statement that he considered only obvious. This experience gave him an opportunity to rethink his worldview.

It is the public (that is, the public attitude toward war crimes and war responsibility), treacherous journalists, and pseudointellectuals who changed. They are the ones who allowed the assassination attempt to materialize. It was not, "We cannot let the mayor become a hero," but it was actually "We cannot let the mayor become prominent." Motojima Hitoshi, the mayor of Nagasaki, is already a minor hero of the Japanese political scene. He would not be a hero in Germany or Italy, since he would merely be stating the obvious. But here a person whose only feat was not to change his view on the Emperor since the end of the war could be seen as a courageous hero.

The January 24, 1990, issue of *Asahi Shinbun* carries an article titled, "Violence Against Freedom of Speech: The Isolated and Helpless Victims," which reports on the vulnerable and isolated people who are threatened and victimized by the violence of right-wing thugs. If things proceed as they have for quite a while, we will have no more "heroes" in the future; or freedom of speech will be eliminated so that even heroes of this type will disappear. If journalists have reflected upon the implications of the assassination attempt for free speech, then in order not to produce any more heroes they should resume the kind of reporting that would successfully challenge various taboos such as the Emperor's war crime— precisely by vigorously using freedom of speech (though this cannot be expected from many of our corrupt journalists).

Once upon a time, the Nobel Prize Committee awarded the Nobel Peace Prize to [Satô Eisaku] the younger brother of the now-deceased former Prime Minister Kishi Nobusuke, who was a Class A war criminal. Of course, just because one is genetically related to someone does not mean that one's beliefs and values are the same. But in this case, he was not just anyone whose values conflicted with those of his brother's. In order to recover the tainted credibility of the Nobel Prize caused by their decision to honor Kishi's brother, why doesn't the committee award the prize to Motojima to criticize Japan's single-party dictatorship and its conformist society, just as it did with the previous year's prize-winner, the Dalai Lama?

1990

The Failures
of the International PEN Congress

In 1984, the International PEN Congress was held in Tokyo for about a week. PEN is a group for writers. The Japanese chapter has some 1,000 members. The first head was Shimazaki Tôson; currently it is Inoue Yasushi.* PEN upholds various ideals, including freedom of expression and the need to work for world peace.

Last year, I joined the Japanese PEN chapter, so I attended the international conference eagerly. The morning joint session was entitled "Literature in the Nuclear Age: Why Do We Write?" In the afternoon, I attended a session on writers and human rights.

In conclusion, it was a great disappointment. I had thought that the congress was a place to debate issues, but in reality it is a place to lecture. Indeed, in most of the lectures there was nary a chance to ask questions.

---

*Shimakaki and Inoue are both novelists.

During the opening ceremony, Inoue stated that the conference was a forum to freely debate issues. However, before the first lecture by Endô Shûsaku, the master of ceremonies explicitly asked the listeners not to make any statement or raise any questions. "If you have questions, please ask them on a personal basis during the rest period." Is this what a master of ceremonies should do? Is his function to prevent debate and discussion? How is it possible to uphold the freedom of expression touted by Inoue?

Why did I, and many others, participate? We were all just listeners—so many props. As a prop, one might at least get a fee, but we had to pay a large sum to attend the conference. If we were just going to listen, why don't they simply distribute the speeches in printed form?

At PEN conferences abroad—Caracas, Lyon, Rio de Janeiro, or Stockholm—there is no instance in which people's participation was curbed. Time runs out, but no bureaucratic writer exists who mechanically closes the session on time. As a writer from the United States told me, "It is nonsensical to have a conference without any discussion." Of course, without any debate, there is no confusion. Perhaps this was a reflection of the Japanese bureaucratic spirit. Many participants in the 1964 Tokyo Olympics complained because the officials were concerned with bureaucratic matters, championing punctuality and order above all else.

The second failure was the paucity of participants from the third world. In particular, no black African came, and no African American writer from the United States appeared. Presumably, these writers had other things to do. In retrospect, it was really a good thing that they didn't come. If someone had come all the way from Senegal, for example, the writer would have been thoroughly angered by the lack of opportunity to discuss issues.

There is no real way to find out why third world writers overlooked the Tokyo conference unless we ask them directly. However, one possibility was its political emphasis—which was anti-third world. The title of the conference was apparently debated at length: either "Literature in the Nuclear Age" or "Literature under Nuclear Threat." Because the latter was considered too "political," the former, more neutral, title was selected. This "nonpolitical" emphasis belies, however, its deeply political nature. Third world writers do not have the luxury of discussing the "nuclear age." They are forced to live under the conditions created by the so-called advanced countries—not just nuclear threat but economic threat as well.

And there is a third failure. Although various writers mentioned Hiroshima and Nagasaki, Auschwitz, Stalin, the plague in medieval Europe, Dresden, and the street children of Brazil, no one mentioned the Cambodian massacre. Pol Pot's genocidal action resulted in up to 4 million deaths. Although the Cambodian massacre is of much greater impact and scale than Hiroshima or Nagasaki, no one bothered to say a word about it, even though it concerns an event quite close to Tokyo.

Fourth, many people criticize Japan for being sensitive to its victimization but not to its aggression. Although there was a panel on "Writers and Human Rights," the topic was discussed in terms of the writers' victimization. No one questioned the writers' "responsibility" or "aggression." For example, it is not possible to question writers who collaborate with the publishing house Bungei Shunjû, which is thoroughly anti-antinuclear.

As a Korean-Japanese writer, Ri Kaisei, warned, the International PEN Conference is "a place for European and North American writers to socialize intellectually. At best, it is a ceremony to satisfy intellectual curiosity through cultural exchange."

In the farewell party on the last day of the conference, a symbolic event occurred. The orchestra turned up its volume such that conversation became impossible. Surprised, many people had to leave the hall to continue their conversation. I went to the stage to ask the orchestra to lower the volume, but in the absence of anyone in charge, my request was denied. Thus the international PEN meeting prevented "expression" to the last moment.

1984

IV
The Archipelago of Ecological Disasters

Disfigured Tadpoles

When my father died, I took a leave of absence from my company and returned to my village in Shinshû, where my mother and my physically disabled sister still lived. One summer day, I went to catch tadpoles for the pond in our backyard. The image of tadpoles swimming to and fro symbolized the beautiful and peaceful village of my childhood. I wanted to recreate that image in the pond that I had made with my father when I was in junior high school.

Twenty meters or so from our house, there is a steep slope. At the bottom there is a swamp. Here and there are rivulets and puddles, creating a haven for fish, small animals, and insects. In Fabre's *Entomological Souvenirs*, there are beautiful passages describing Fabre's plains, but the swamp of my childhood transfixed us as youngsters. From the end of World War II to the postwar period of food scarcity, this swamp has gradually been turned into rice paddies. These days, between the finished barriers and organized aqueducts, the swamp of my youth has virtually vanished.

Nonetheless, that alone should not have prevented me from finding tadpoles. As in the past, water still flows and tadpoles can live in rice paddy. But pesticides have wreaked havoc—I could not find a single tadpole. Except for eels, all the fish that used to be so plentiful have disappeared. From my childhood memory and play, I know very well which type of fish live in which part of the small river. Therefore, it didn't take me long to realize that there were no tadpoles in all the swamp. Shrimp, like tadpoles, have also completely died out.

It seems possible that tadpoles have disappeared completely from our village. I asked the village radio station to help me find some tadpoles. The day after the broadcast, my mother pointed to a bucket and said, "Look, people brought you tadpoles." A youth from a neighboring hamlet had brought them to me. I looked into the bucket—into a sad reality. They were not tadpoles but minnows. The youth in our village can longer tell tadpoles from other creatures. Finally, we decided that there were no tadpoles at all in our village.

Three days later, an acquaintance told me about one place nearby where there were tadpoles. My mother, my friend, and I went there with nets to catch some tadpoles. My mother enjoyed fishing and mushroom hunting more than anything else.

There were definitely tadpoles there. It was a very small river, less than two feet in width. There are no other rivers nearby. The reason is simple. The small river was formed by the waste of a nearby electric generation plant. Plunging into the river, we caught a lot of tadpoles, chubs, and carp. In a short time, we caught over two hundred tadpoles and the bucket was full. "Let's go home," I said. My mother began to take a few steps but returned to the river smiling, "One more time," she said.

When I put the tadpoles into the pond, my hometown was recreated. Tadpoles break up into three or four groups and swim to and fro. Other fish swim near the bottom, but tadpoles always swim near the surface.

As I was watching the tadpoles, I was shocked that a good number of them had twisted backs—perhaps one in seven or eight. It must be from the pollution. Where the pesticides were stronger, the tadpoles died. Where the poison was weaker, these survived but were deformed. I had not recreated my original hometown at all, but rather a warped and distorted version of it.

Two months later, a day before she was to visit my uncle in Kyushu, my mother died. She collapsed right after packing. I will never forget my mother's smile as she said "One more time" when we went to catch tadpoles for the last time.

Without my parents, my village is a lonely place. If the rivers were still filled with shrimp and tadpoles, if the fireflies still flew into the house, if the frogs still cried all night long, our village would still encompass the images and smell of my parents. Such a place would evoke my home. But our beautiful and verdant village has become silent because of the terrible poisoning of our mountains and farms. With my parents' death, nature also died. Not sadness but anger dwells within.

One year after my mother died, I could no longer find any disfigured tadpoles in our pond. In a pond without pesticides, the new generation revived, producing healthy tadpoles. The principle is simple: stop the pollution. However, such a simple principle is never enacted by our government. When antipollution legislation is passed, it becomes gutted. In the case of the tadpoles' spines, rapid generational change seems to be a cure, but the same cannot be said for children who were disabled by Minamata.* Our bodies are increasingly polluted.

I was in North Vietnam two years after my mother's death. When I walked through the villages, all the paddies and rivers were full of shrimp and small fish. The farmers were trying not to sacrifice these organisms and were using a type of water plant as fertilizer. The villagers discussed their resolve not to use chemical fertilizers, which are harmful to human beings.

As I was looking at the small fish in the paddies, I wondered who was being destroyed. North Vietnam is daily being bombed and destroyed. However, the country that is being more fundamentally destroyed is Japan. My village can be seen in North Vietnamese villages. With the plan for the renovation of the Japanese archipelago, what will happen to our nature and environment? In my hometown, new highway construction is in progress. People even discuss a new high-speed railway system. I wonder if the villagers will really find happiness in all this.

1973

---

*Minamata was perhaps the most celebrated case of a pollution-related disease in postwar Japan.

Vanishing Ptarmigan

I am concerned that ptarmigan have disappeared from the Kiso mountains. The first time I climbed the central alps was in my second year of high school in October 1949. I am particularly fond of these mountains and have climbed them about ten times along four different routes since that first trip. My most recent attempt was in 1976.

I noticed something was amiss a few years ago. I no longer encountered ptarmigan, which were always present along the ridgelines. As I walked along the ridge, ptarmigan would take off from creeping pine trees and fly low and close to the ground, then hover for a short while in the fog, struggling against the strong winds rising upward from the Kiso side, and disappear in the direction of our destination. On sunny days, ptarmigan never showed themselves for fear of *hayabusa* [peregrine falcon] and *kumataka* [Hodgson's hawk eagle]. Ptarmigan would almost always appear unless it was sunny. When we became tired of walking, the appearance of the friendly bird was always a welcome sight, and we would invariably lay down our gear and gaze at them in fascination.

Such incidents ceased to take place a few years ago, or possibly a decade ago. As for last year's climb, even though it rained during the entire two days, not a single ptarmigan appeared, nor did we once hear its distinctive cry. I must assume that the ptarmigan of the central alps have faced the dark fate of extinction.

In the case of the central alps, the number of climbers in these regions has increased dramatically since a cable car was built. The waves of climbers are having an impact in the central region. On the other hand, in the area further south, the increase has not been significant since the ascent is treacherous. Despite the fact that the southern area is visited by fewer hikers, I have not seen ptarmigan there either in the last few years. Therefore, in the northern area, where there have been more climbers, the possibility of the ptarmigan's survival looks very slim. Most likely, ptarmigan have vanished from the central alps. Since many of the romantic and happy memories of my younger days are intimately associated with these mountains, the extinction of the ptarmigan pains me so much that I feel as if part of my youth has been chipped away.

There are several hypotheses concerning the ptarmigan's departure. Because of the numerous climbers who dump their garbage, the number of pests such as rats has begun to increase in the high mountains. Foxes and other animals that prey on those small rodents have also grown in number. Simultaneously, predators have been chased out of the foothills by the indiscriminate cutting of trees and the spraying of agricultural pesticides, and have moved up the mountains, thereby preying on the ptarmigan.

For a long time, I have been enraged by Japan's forest management policy. The present plight of the ptarmigan in the central alps has confirmed my belief that Japan's forest management policy is irresponsible and destructive. The true enemy of ptarmigan is the government's forest management policy.

1977

Why Resorts?

People who grew up in the countryside should go back and observe the mountains and rivers of your youth. People who grew up near the ocean, observe your favorite beach. People who grew up in a city, revisit a rural area you visited several years ago. You will then understand the continuing destruction of our environment. Yet the present is better than the future. During the Nakasone regime, the Diet passed a "resort" law. It is something one expects from the Liberal Democratic Party, but other parties and the media failed to oppose the passage of this odious legislation.

I visited the Shiga Highlands near my hometown recently. The mountains have become bald from all the ski slopes. Even the last bastion of nature, the national park, is threatened with "development." Tourist companies, including Seibu,* are lined up with development plans. Furthermore, construction

---

*Seibu is a large conglomerate, best known for fancy department stores.

is paid for with public money as corporations negotiate favorable financial arrangements. My hometown is being invaded.

What is the meaning of progress in this seemingly prosperous country? Even as the environmental problem is becoming the pressing issue facing humanity, the forestry department is cutting down old-growth forest in national parks, and the Ministry of the Environment supports plans to destroy the last remaining coral reef to build an airport in Okinawa.

Currently, the "resort plan" is to turn over 20 percent—not 2 but 20—of the Japanese land area to golf courses and other types of leisure development.

There is nothing more destructive to land than golf courses. Forests and trees are destroyed, while pesticides and herbicides endanger our drinking water. Moreover, the invading economy leads to the destruction of the regional economy and the collapse of local human relations. Villagers are tantamount to slaves of the invading urban developers. They become the modern "primitives."

The same destructive effect occurs in the construction of ski slopes. Highway construction and the artificial manufacture of snow take a terrible toll on the land.

What has happened to our archipelago? Some argue that the Japanese value nature, but I have my doubts. It is true that there are sites of natural beauty in Japan. However, the people who live on the land are, sadly, devoid of any desire to be grateful for, and prevent the destruction of, nature. There are only 20,000 people in bird-watching societies, but over 300,000 people have licenses to shoot these birds.

Japan is populated by some of the most spiritually impoverished people in the world. How sad for the archipelago.

1989

"Development" as Invasion

So far, no one has bought up the atmosphere. Yet it is possible to enclose a particular area and claim all the air within. This is no longer a matter of fantasy; that is precisely what is happening to water and land.

I could say the same about almost everywhere, but let's consider North America. Until the European invaders arrived, the land belonged to the people who lived there: the Native Americans and Inuit. More important, land was not private property; it belonged to the community. Now, however, except for a few national parks and forests, all the land belongs to individuals or corporations. How did this happen?

The simplest method of acquiring land was just to take it. However, the fighting capacity of the Native Americans was considerable, so it was not as easy as that. Hence, the invaders stole it through treaties. These treaties were made with tribal leaders. The invaders threatened or seduced a leader and forced him to give up the land. Thus land that did not even belong to the leader became the private property of the invaders without the others' consent. The invaders showed the treaty to the angry people, claimed "legality," and threw the people out.

What happened when a leader did not sign? Sometimes, invaders found a corruptible person and made him the chief; they created a puppet. Then the treaty was made with him and the land was stolen. Of course, real leaders often got angry and waged war, but the U.S. military forcefully put down such uprisings and sometimes massacred the people.

What happened when village solidarity was so strong that no puppet leader came forward? The invaders signed a treaty with a neighboring people who had lost their land; the invaders took the land by treaty with people who were not involved. In such a case, fighting was ferocious, but the people lost to modern weaponry and to invaders.

The history of the United States is a series of such horrible invasions. Most presidents were directly involved in this terrible process.

Tanaka's "real estate" cabinet is doing the same thing in Japan.* The Japanese people who farm and fish have become the indigenous people. Let's look at the example of Tomatô in Hokkaido.

The plain to the east of Tomatô was once a large forest. After all the trees were cut down by manufacturers of pulp, furniture, and matches, the area was cultivated as farmland by pioneering farmers. The current plan is to turn this farm-

---

*Tanaka Kakuei was prime minister of Japan in the early 1970s. He was best known for his plan to "reform the Japanese archipelago" *(nihon rettô kaizô)* and his involvement in the Lockheed scandal.

land—and the public river and beach—over to large corporations.

Take the river, for example. The corporation plans to create a dam to obtain the water necessary for factories. Although all the farmers are involved, the corporation is negotiating only with the farmers whose land will be underwater when the proposed dam is built. All is well as long as a treaty is made with this minority of farmers.

Take the ocean, for another example. Troublemakers are engaged in fishing. Hence, a treaty is made with these people. Thus, the public beach is bought up as a corporate harbor or for oil storage; we may no longer "trespass" on this area.

In this manner, Tomatô has been bought up. It is now a ghost town. The only thing that concerns the people is the problem of pollution. The invasion of the developers was never questioned. Mayors and city council members gladly fulfilled the role of puppets.

1974

Why Dolphins?

Some Japanese fishermen at Katsumoto in Oki Island, Nagasaki Prefecture, became annoyed by dolphins, which were wreaking havoc in the excellent yellowtail and squid fishing ground. The fishermen chased herds of dolphins into a net on the shore. Dexter Kate, a thirty-six-year-old American who is a member of an animal rights organization, freed the dolphins by cutting the net. Charges were brought against Kate, and the so-called Dolphin Trial is still going on at the Sasebo Branch of the Nagasaki District Court. The discussion at the court so far has mainly dealt with a technical issue (whether the incident happened inside or outside a national park), and little argument has been made on the essence of this incident.

The significance of this incident is more than "a battle between fishermen and animal rights activists over dolphins." I visited Americans who stayed in Sasebo to support Kate and participated in discussions that often lasted until midnight. I also went to Sasebo Prison and talked with Kate personally (even though journalists are not supposed to talk with the accused). Katsumoto Fishery Cooperative in Oki Island let me visit and collect information on their position as well.

At an inn in Sasebo I met three Americans from Hawaii who supported Kate. They were Susan Kate, his wife; Bruce Kate, his brother; and Keith Klueger, a television producer who specializes in environmental issues. Susan Kate had her one-year-old baby with her.

"Why dolphins?" was the key question in my discussion with the accused and his supporters. Why is it necessary to protect dolphins above all other animals, even by invading another country's sovereignty?

Generally speaking, wildlife protection is undertaken for two reasons: first, when wildlife directly benefits human beings (for example, the swallow and the mongoose); second, when an animal or plant is rare and under threat of extinction (for example, the Japanese crested ibis and the great salamander).

There are certainly rare kinds of dolphins in the world, but the dolphins living around Oki Island are not in danger of extinction. Approximately 300,000 dolphins exist in the northern Kyushu area, and according to Dr. Mizue Kazuhiro, a professor at the Institute of Marine Science at Tokyo University, the population of dolphins in these oceans cannot withstand further increase.

Do dolphins benefit human beings, then? The answer differs from place to place. The country that has obviously profited the most in the world is the United States, which has also killed the largest number of dolphins. Americans developed a method of finding tuna by using dolphins. The Japanese tuna fishing method, on the other hand, does not hurt dolphins directly. On the contrary, dolphins fight with fishermen over yellowtail and squid, as we have seen around Oki Island. In a sense, the dolphin has been regarded as a harmful animal in Japan, although it has also been one of the edible creatures in the ocean.

Thus, it is difficult to observe a generally accepted principle for wildlife protection in the case of dolphins around Oki Island. I therefore began my interview with the American animal rights activists by asking why dolphins should be protected. They answered first that any animal has a right to life, and that fishermen have no right to kill dolphins just because that is how they make their living. This may be true, but the logic also applies to any animal, not only to dolphins. What is so special about dolphins, then? The activists claimed that there is little need to kill dolphins, that it is human beings who expanded their fishing ground and invaded the dolphins' territory as fishing methods became more advanced. They added that the destruction of marine ecology by the pollution on the coastline might have caused the dolphins to become more aggressive. Certainly, ecological destruction is a serious matter. I would think, however, that ecology is about all living creatures, and not only about dolphins. The activists' argument still does not specify the particular reason for saving these dolphins.

The activists responded: "We could no longer tolerate the fishermen's brutal killing of dolphins. Many dolphins were speared in front of their friends, and the water turned red with their blood." The activists showed me a documentary movie recording the dolphin slaughter to prove their point. I still wondered, however, whether killing dolphins would be justified if fishermen were to slaughter each dolphin in a separate room. (I also think that the concept of brutality differs from place to place.) The activists provided little counterargument; instead, they stressed that the dolphin has a developed brain and high intelligence and thus never harms human beings. The language such as "developed brain" and "high intelligence" indicates the reference point of the activists' logic in according a privileged place to dolphins. Kate, the accused man in this court case, stated that although we have to consider all lives equally, the dolphin is highly intelligent and shares many features with human beings. In short, the dolphin is distinctive for its brain.

This raises a question of how we determine the dolphin's level of intelligence. How could we prove that the dolphin is intelligent enough to demand to be treated almost like a human being? Is there an exceptionally large discrepancy between dolphin intelligence and that of other sea animals (for example, seals, which are slaughtered for their fur in Alaska) or cows and chimpanzees? The activists gave me a scholarly article that compares the brain size, the degree of convolution, and number of brain cells of *Homo sapiens,* orangutans, dogs, monkeys, and dolphins. Among the activists, however, there was no agreement on the distinctive difference in intellectual capacity between dolphins and other animals. Susan Kate thinks that there is no critical difference between dolphins and other animals, whereas Bruce Kate claims that there is. Bruce even said that killing a dolphin is as bad as killing a human being. He also stated that a cow's intelligence may well be the same as a dog's.

Whether this distinction between dolphins and other animals is valid or not, a more important issue is why no question arises on killing animals of lesser intelligence. Why can we slaughter cows without any problem? The activists provided no justification to explain less-intelligent animals' destiny, while they rationalized that cows can be controlled as livestock and therefore we can slaughter them. I asked them whether we can domesticate dolphins and then slaughter them. Their response was in effect that this would be pathetic and barbaric. Their argument is not logical but rather emotional, deeply rooted in their own history and culture.

For those born and raised in Western culture, dolphins and whales are animals that frequently appear in ancient Greek or Roman mythology. A comparable animal in India is the cow, which is regarded as sacred and has never become livestock for slaughter and consumption. Thus, the difference in cultural or historical background is significant.

Such an understanding of cultural and historical differences does not erase one question, however. Why it is only Americans who travel a long way to Japan to cut fishing nets to protest the killing of dolphins, and not Indians who attack Hokkaido's ranches and set the cows free? I asked them what they would think if Indians went to ranches in the western United States and liberated the cows. Susan simply replied: "They are free to do so, so let them do it." My next question— What if the Indians broke down the fences of the ranches and freed the cows?—received no response from them.

Japanese in the United States who have directly experienced the West would know the consequence of such activities. The Indians who practiced such things would definitely be killed (through private sanction). One of the fundamental problems is this: it is Americans who come to Japan to rescue dolphins, not Indians, Vietnamese, Germans, or French. American activists (including Kate) with the best of intentions hardly realize that their thinking has been deeply influenced by the ideology of American political, military, religious, and cultural hegemony in the world.

On the other hand, the Japanese reacted to this incident with a logic that was in no way persuasive to the Americans. For example, they pointed out America's past cruelty to wildlife, including the passenger pigeon, the buffalo, and the whale. In fact, it was for whale hunting ships that the United States demanded that the Tokugawa government open up Japan.* Some Japanese also argue that the prosperity of Oki Island's coastal whale fishery suffered because the United States caught almost all the whales in the late Tokugawa and early Meiji periods. This is all true, but it is a matter of the past. Currently, the United States does protect wildlife (including whales) far more seriously than Japan.

Another criticism of the United States is that Americans use a method of catching tuna that kills several times more dolphins than Japanese fishermen do. This is true, too, although the situation is rapidly changing. According to the U.S. National Tropical Tuna Committee, the number of slaughtered dolphins has gradually decreased owing to a series of protection laws. Until around 1972, more than 300,000 dolphins were killed each year, while last year the number dropped to 16,000. The way in which they counted killed dolphins raises a bit of suspicion over accuracy, but the rapidly decreasing number seems true. Fishing methods as well as fishing nets have been improved, too. It may not take too long to reduce the number of killed dolphins to near zero.

---

*During the Tokugawa period (1603–1868), Japan ceased almost all contact with foreign governments and traders.

Some Japanese critics also questioned the weight placed on human and dolphin life, saying that human beings are more important than dolphins, and that Americans should protest racism in the United States and the indiscriminate massacre by the U.S. military force in Vietnam. This kind of argument does not make sense to the radical activists fighting to protect nature, for they *did* protest the Vietnam war as well as nuclear bomb testing and nuclear power plants.

In the most calm and logical manner, another American made a case for two points: first, the problem is ultimately the destruction of the environment, which will hurt fishermen later; and second, we have to prevent this planet from being destroyed by human beings. This is a fair argument, except that it does not explain why only dolphins among all creatures should be privileged. Eventually, the focus returns to "intelligence."

As I examined various aspects of the activists' ideas, I found their argument weak in three respects. The first is their understanding of dolphin's intelligence in comparison with that of other animals. We should be cautious. The way animals are ranked based on their intelligence is very similar to the way Japanese children with various talents are judged and ranked by their score on college entrance exams, the single measurement defined by the Ministry of Education. Second, even if we admit the hypothesis the dolphin is the smartest animal of all, the activists' argument does not explain why other animals that rank lower than dolphins do not have to be rescued. When I saw the activists compare the quality of brain, I could not help recalling the way in which the Nazis used physical anthropology to argue for the superiority of the German nation. The third problem with their argument is, as I have already indicated, their arrogance based on the hegemonic power of the United States.

What is the argument of the fishermen on Oki Island? Well, it is very clear and simple: "Dolphins are an enemy and an obstacle to our fishing business." One of the employees at Katsumoto Fishery Cooperative murmured that the dolphins used to come in a herd and that fishermen simply had to pass around them. Today, in contrast, dolphins spread around the fishery ground, and each fishing boat is always attended by a few dolphins which aim at the yellowtail and squid caught in the fishermen's net. Thus, a major determinant of a yield per boat really depends on whether the boat has attending dolphins or not. In fact, the yield clearly increases for about two days after the dolphins are chased into the net. The cooperative employee complained that "people do not understand the real situation very well; the fisherman's livelihood is threatened by dolphins. Which is more pitiful, dolphins or fishermen? We actually do not want to kill them. We have tried everything to chase them out, but nothing has worked. I would like to tell the activists to take all the dolphins to American coasts or wherever." The fishermen's hatred of the dolphins is strong. I even heard that when fishermen see dolphins, they feel like jumping into the ocean, fighting with the dolphins and killing them.

If we think about this particular dolphin problem around Oki Island, this fishermen's argument is much more persuasive than that of the activists. Does this mean that these American activists have to leave Japan discouraged? Should they be stoned and driven away from Japan, and then stay in Hawaii and fight against the discrimination of Polynesians or the environmental destruction of Micronesia caused by nuclear experiments and the presence of U.S. military bases? Does Japan have nothing to reflect on in this incident?

The question that should be raised here is not the specifics of this incident, such as dolphins or fishermen in Oki Island, but rather the general concern with the environment. If Japan had actively dealt with various environmental problems and taken a leadership role in environmental protection in the world, it could have explained its particular concerns about this incident and convinced other people much more easily. However, in reality, the exact opposite pertains. The Japanese archipelago is like a world exhibition of various forms of pollution and environmental destruction. A recent example is the April 16 decision of the Kumamoto District Court. This court decision virtually gave permission to proceed with the mercury sludge disposal project at Minamata Bay—the site of the internationally infamous Minamata disease (mercury poisoning)—despite citizens' appeals against the project's potential risk to human health. The environmental assessment law effectively shut out expert testimony from the public hearings by strictly defining witnesses as "citizens." The government convinced unsophisticated (or ignorant) citizens with the power of the developers' computer.

Of course, the government's attitude is not the only indicator of Japan's backwardness in environmental protection. While some birds such as the *toki* get enthusiastic attention because they are a curiosity, the public interest in wild birds is amazingly low. In contrast, the sounds of shotguns are heard everywhere in the forests in winter. Doves in parks and temples receive generous love, but unfortunately, doves are harmful to human life while most wild birds benefit us. According to the Japan Wild Bird Association, there are only

9,500 people in Japan who belong to any organization for the protection of wild birds, whereas there are 376,000 in the United States and 386,000 in Britain. The huge gap between Japan and Western countries is pathetic. Another example: Last year, the ban on antelope hunting was partially lifted because of the belief that the increase in the number of antelopes harmed human life, although some scholars (for example, the director of the Japan Monkey Center)* have presented a strong objection to such a view.

In the United States, *The China Syndrome* with Jane Fonda was successful; it received some positive reviews and also succeeded in making a profit, despite the movie's opposition to nuclear power plants and its critique of U.S. capitalism. I doubt that any famous Japanese actress would become involved in producing such a movie, nor would there be a Japanese audience to make such a movie successful.

What I have argued is that the problem with the dolphins should be a chance for Japan to reflect on its own problems with the environment in general, even if Japanese fishermen have a better argument than the activists in this particular incident. It is Japan's general attitude to the environment with which this incident should be concerned. At the same time, U.S. activists, including Kate, must realize that their actions are based on illogical, ethnocentric ideas, which are supported by U.S. hegemony, and that they are simply provoking resentment among the Japanese.

1980

---

*The Monkey Center studies wild animals in general.

V
The Politics
of Single-Party Dictatorship

Japanese "Democracy":
The Oldest Single-Party Dictatorship

Last November, a visiting French judge stressed to me the importance of changing political administrations. Since 1981, when the Socialist Party came to power in France, significant changes have occurred in court judgments. Judges who made sycophantic judgments to curry favor with the previous administration find themselves in uncomfortable positions. To avoid this, judges must strive to make judgments independent of political considerations, and judgments become more just.

This would have ocurred in Japan if the separation of the three branches of government (administrative, legislative, and judicial) functioned according to design. However, the separation has become dysfunctional. The judicial branch ingratiates itself with the ruling Liberal Democratic Party.

The courts have been making senseless judgments, such as the indictment regarding the authorization of textbooks.[*]

---

[*] Honda refers to a court case dealing with government censorship of history texts dealing with Japan's role in World War II.

Although we can enjoy some pathetic humor from judges who have totally renounced their moral fiber and pride and are anxiously serving the powers that be, as citizens of a law-abiding nation we are forced to obey these judges, however pitiful they are. Our disdainful, puppetlike courts of law will, however, be forced to transform themselves when a change of administration takes place.

Based on last year's "historical" election of the Upper House, Japan has moved a half step forward to the possibility of changing the regime in power.* Who is most afraid of change? Of course, corporations closely tied to the Nakasone-Recruit administration are afraid. They have made gargantuan profit through scandalous "legalized" corruption. They continue to fatten themselves by gobbling up people's tax money, although they themselves always find ways to avoid taxation. However, the people whose eyes are truly filled with fear and who are praying desperately that there will be no change of regime are the mainstream governmental bureaucrats and judicial officials. They have profited and promoted themselves with their all-out adulation of the ruling party.

I asked an opposition party member who was elected for the first time in this "historical" election what her impression of politics was since she had been elected six months ago. "First," she said, "I have become convinced that the kind of structural corruption that Japan presently suffers from will never be eradicated unless a change of the entire regime takes place." Although I have heard enough examples to feed a horse (examples that all testify to the correctness of her

*In the Upper House election of 1989, the Liberal Democrats lost their outright majority.

analysis), here I will limit myself to the kind of "information" the government monopolizes. Compared to the United States, where the separation of the three branches is functioning at least somewhat better than in Japan, we have very few pieces of legislation proposed by Diet members. For the most part we have laws that were originally proposed by the administrative branch of the government. Although we have "review sessions," they are nothing more than rituals to complete the procedure. The best that one can expect from opposition parties is a supplementary resolution. The postwar Japanese Diet is essentially no different from the prewar Imperial Diet. To be sure, Diet members proposed a considerable number of laws immediately after World War II, apparently as a result of the guidance provided by the U.S. occupation force.

The most significant cause of the present situation is that over the long span of domination by a single party, members of the leading Liberal Democratic Party and government bureaucrats developed extremely close relations. Eventually, the party and the government bureaucracies formed a system in which every important decision was arrived at by mutual consent. In short, the separation of the three branches of government collapsed in postwar Japan. One exemplary symptom is government control of information. Despite their legal obligation to submit information to all political parties, the bureaucracy often relays important information to the LDP alone. Far from the full disclosure of information to the public, the government bureaucrats discriminate against non-LDP Diet members, who also supposedly represent the people. This is a profoundly disturbing and illegal situation.

Japan needs a *glasnost*, perhaps even more than the Soviet Union. For instance, let us recall a bill to abolish the consumption tax that the opposition Socialist Party introduced. The LDP and the Ministry of Finance attacked the Socialist Party for errors they found in the bill, but the errors were only a natural and logical consequence of the present political structure. The complexity of legislative activity ensures that numerous errors will emerge even if the Finance Ministry itself produces the bill. Opposition parties face even greater problems since they have no access to the very information needed to formulate legislation. On the other hand, from the viewpoint of the LDP members, they do not wish to consider questions regarding the availability of information when any bill can be produced by "mutual consent" between the LDP and the bureaucrats.

A similar corrupt situation can be seen in the office of ODA [Official Development Assistance—government aid to third world countries]. For instance, according to the official ODA estimate, ¥15 billion [about $120 million] was allocated to build a power plant in the Philippines. It is impossible to investigate where the money came from, how it was handled during the process, or how it was finally spent. All the costs are reported only in aggregates. Attempts to obtain a detailed account of project expenditure are frustrated. The investigator encounters various barriers such as "classified diplomacy," "corporate secrets," or "interference with internal affairs"—all designed to make it impossible for an outsider to trace the use of funds. However, if one looks at the results of the so-called aid, one finds numerous abuses. For example, some aid takes the form of "reflexive aid," designed ultimately to benefit corporations. Aid sometimes also results in gross violation of human rights or environmental destruction. Such immoral use of foreign aid is already established at the institutional level, so it would be impossible to make any change in aid procedure through Diet deliberations. Why? In the national budget, the only items that are open to deliberation are general public accounts, special accounts, and government-related agency accounts. Public corporations and industries are exempt from government control. Thus, ODA becomes a hotbed of corruption. According to *Shûkan Post* [a popular weekly], which has been waging a vigorous campaign of criticism against ODA corruption, ODA has "thrown the Philippine economy into a debt hell." Opposition parties are advocating the establishment of a basic legal framework for ODA, requiring it to go through the deliberation process in the National Assembly. However, unless there is a change of regime, ODA will remain a hotbed of malfeasance.

Japan's opposition parties have been incapacitated by the long period of LDP dictatorship which spreads the corrupt regime's net of economic interests over local governments throughout Japan. The bitterness of the opposition parties is wholeheartedly shared by the aforementioned first-year member of the Upper House:

> The Diet must be transformed. The present state of the government, in which the Diet is controlled through the collaboration of LDP politicians, bureaucrats, and financiers, will never lead to "parliamentary democracy."

> If the present regime collapses, ministers elected from the opposition parties will, without hesitation, be able to order bureaucracies to submit all necessary information concerning government expenditure such as ODA. Bureaucracy is not the essence of politics. Politics is supposed to be about informed leadership. The Diet is the forum for discussing and deciding which actions Japan as a nation should take and how the national budget should be decided. Bureaucracies are institutions designed to execute the results of policy

deliberation. Scandals involving the LDP, such as Recruit or Lockheed, occurred because we have lost the necessary separation of the three branches of government and everything is now decided behind closed doors.

The Recruit and Lockheed cases are just the tip of the iceberg. The present structure makes corruption inevitable. This has nothing to do with capitalism, socialism, or any other political ideology. If a single-party dictatorship is allowed to continue long enough, a nation will produce a Marcos or a Ceausescu. Issues like the consumption tax or the liberalization of rice imports are important, of course, but first and foremost we must regain our parliamentary democracy and reaffirm the separation of the three branches of government. This is the most urgent issue for Japanese politics today.

We have witnessed *perestroika* sweeping the Soviet Union and Eastern Europe, long considered the world's most entrenched single-party dictatorships. It appears, however, that Japan may soon become a nation with the longest history of single-party dictatorship. Is it possible that the level of corruption in Japan is proportionally the highest in the world? It is clear that the core of the problem lies in the lack of change of regime. However, the Liberal Democratic Party fraudulently projects the same old East-West conflict paradigm and adheres to the outdated Cold War framework. Historically, fascist regimes have always been good at this sort of demagogy and scapegoating.

1990

Prime Minister Nakasone as Nazisone

Prime Minister Nakasone Yasuhiro continues to embarrass us. When he deplored the "low knowledge level of Americans," I immediately sensed that it would become a very serious controversy. However, some journalists who worked as special correspondents in the United States for many years disagreed with my view. Is this an example of the low Japanese "knowledge level" in regard to the United States, a country with a large population of oppressed minorities? The *Washington Post* expressed its amazement at the Japanese mass media for not taking the incident seriously.

Many Japanese believe that knowledge is merely accumulated information. They still do not understand that even though their grade school children enjoy the highest average test scores in the world, students' competence declines in high school and college. A friend who just returned from the United States told me that a large number of the young Japanese scholars who are in the United States to pursue postdoctoral studies are totally incompetent. For many decades, Japan's Ministry of Education has been discouraging students from thinking individually and critically. Perhaps this is a natural consequence in a country where gossip sheets masquerade as magazines, and enjoy large circulations. Even their victims do nothing but quietly swallow the insults. In this world one rarely finds a nation more ignorant of its conduct during World War II than Japan, so much so that we have nonchalantly elected a war criminal to be prime minister [former Prime Minister Kishi Nobusuke] and now quietly approve Nakasone's visit to Yasukuni Shrine. Nakasone's true colors are also apparent from his statements during his presidency of Takushoku University, a well-known right-wing institution. His thinking is deeply militaristic; perhaps the Japanese people have not noticed it because of their "low knowledge level."

In order to vindicate himself, Nakasone revealed himself to be Nazisone when he stated that "Japan is a homogeneous nation," right after the previous claim. The Ainu, an indigenous Japanese nation and a minority for many centuries, have protested this racist notion believed not only by Nakasone but by the general public in Japan. Nakasone has repeatedly reiterated this racist statement to the public. Even the Ainu people, who have become accustomed to their historical tragedy and ongoing exploitation and oppression and hence rarely express their anger in public, could not maintain their silence this time. The Hokkaido Utari Association decided to send a delegation to the Diet to protest, and the Kanto Utari Association sent an open letter with a set of questions to Nakasone. Nomura Yoshikazu, the chief director of the Hokkaido Utari Association, wrote a letter to *Asahi Shinbun*:

> By claiming Japan to be homogeneous, Nakasone insulted the honor of multiethnic nations around the world.... Although the

Prime Minister discharged the Minister of Education [for making a racist comment in public], given that the Prime Minister is more powerful than the Minister of Education, who will dismiss him?

Opposition parties should get up their nerve and call for the resignation of the Prime Minister and his cabinet.

Let us observe Nakasone's attitude after the mass media reported the Ainu nation's vigorous protest campaign. Responding to the question by LDP Diet member Murakami Masaharu, who had previously requested that the LDP continue its public visit to Yasukuni Shrine (again, a kind of question that only discloses the questioner's "low knowledge level"), Nakasone repeated the nonsense by stating, "In Japan, we have a wonderful asset called national homogeneity." In short, he knowingly ignored the protests of Japan's ethnic minority.

Nakasone's behavior is vividly reminiscent of how Hitler's claims of the superiority of the German nation and the virtue of its racial "purity" were used to justify the extermination of "others" in the gas chamber. It took the colossal sacrifice of World War II to eliminate him from the public stage. Thereafter, the equality of nations (so-called racial equality) became the principle and common goal of the postwar world. The ostentation of national homogeneity is supposed to be a dark memory from the distant past. Nazisone has now brought it back to life in a country in East Asia. What a scandalous, ignorant, and atrocious man we have as our "Prime Minister."

Suppose a country were indeed "nationally homogeneous": Is that such a wonderful asset? Rather, homogeneity should be regarded as a shameful shortcoming. In such a country, people would likely become prone to self-conceit and develop a deformed sense of the international nature of their existence. Nazisone's statement on "knowledge level" is a perfect, concrete example of his isolationist, "anti-international" mentality. No matter how many foreign languages one can speak, no matter how sophisticated and skillful one is socially, if an individual lacks basic consideration for people of different ethnic groups, then she or he cannot claim to be an internationalist, but is rather a "primitive" in the true sense of the word. Our prime minister is an ignorant savage, a caricature of the strange barbarian inhabiting some uncivilized land that never existed. Nazisone-as-savage has never existed in so-called primitive societies. Have we unknowingly elected a man whose civilized standards are far below ours, a man who is an ignorant and ferocious savage? Even though we don't have a method of direct election, since we gave more than three hundred seats in the Diet to the LDP members who are led by this savage, it is a situation we are fully responsible for. Never have we voted "unknowingly." Unfortunately, many Japanese are equally ignorant and fully deserve our bestial prime minister.

My observation can be clarified by comparison with Germany, the very country that gave birth to Nazism. Since I have written about this comparison so many times before, let me simply quote from an essay written by the former chancellor of West Germany, Helmut Schmidt, an essay that was printed in the November 1986 issue of *Sekai*,[*] entitled "Japan Which Has No Friends":

---

[*]*Sekai* is a left-leaning monthly published by Iwanami Shoten; it has a wide readership among intellectuals.

We Germans painfully realized the keen need for analyzing our recent past and future. We then engaged in scrupulous self-criticism, and as a result, we have come to recognize and admit our misdeed. Gradually, even our neighboring countries, which suffered subjugation by Hitler, began to understand our repentance. However, in Southeast Asia, we never hear that Japan engaged in a similar act of self-criticism, or that other Asian countries have decided to accept and trust the present-day, peace-loving Japan.... Japan has no close friends, neither in Asia nor in Europe.... If Japan continues its current self-centered overseas economic policy... not only will the friction regarding the economic and currency reform inevitably intensify between Japan and the United States, Europe, and the newly industrializing countries in East and South Asia, but also Japan may fall into dangerous diplomatic isolation.

I am beginning to be terrified. If ignorant and horrendous Japanese proceed to make Japan into an "unsinkable aircraft carrier" for the sake of the United States, it is possible that Japan will end up as a battlefield, and all human beings on board will be annihilated.* And the rest of the world will not be too sympathetic to the extinction of such a pathetic nation.

1986

---

*Nakasone sought to strengthen Japan's relationship with the United States, especially in the military sphere. Hence, he often employed military metaphors to describe the relationship between the United States and Japan.

Is Prostitution
a Women's Problem?

In 1989, the Liberal Democratic Party suffered a major defeat in the national election for the Upper House. Pundits have ascribed the LDP defeat to women's dissatisfaction with LDP policies. I would guess that women might well be angry with the LDP for the consumption tax, which impoverishes their lives, and the Recruit scandal, which revealed the corruption of the ruling power. Furthermore, at the top of the list is Prime Minister Uno Yûsuke's involvement with a prostitute. Women clearly rejected a politician who still thinks like a feudal landowner. In this sense, 1989 may well be remembered as a turning point in Japanese political history.

Some people believe that Uno had a love affair with a *geisha* and hence did not participate in prostitution. Torikoshi Shuntarô, the chief editor of *Sunday Mainichi*, wrote:

> The woman with whom Uno was involved is equivalent to a high-class call girl. It is true that she used to be a *geisha*; therefore people believe that she is protected by a patron, who would provide her with money and housing, and give her children his name. People, including journalists, tend to have a traditional, sentimental image

of *geisha*. However, in Uno's case, although the woman is called *geisha*, she is simply a call girl who sells her services. There is no love relationship between Uno and the woman—only a monetary relationship. In fact, Uno told her that she should not bear a child, and that she should come to see him only when he calls. This is not a *geisha*-patron relationship, but a prostitute-customer relationship.

It is important to observe the fundamental difference between traditional *geisha* and modern prostitutes. In the Tokugawa period [1603-1868], love affairs outside of marriage were punishable by death; lords, who often had more than one mistress, were excepted. Even after the Meiji restoration [1868], adultery was a crime. In this context, "free" love was only possible with *geisha*, who were available in *yûkaku* [red-light districts]. In the postwar period, when adultery was decriminalized and the Anti-Prostitution Law was passed, men's love relationships with women had different implications. Simply treating a woman as a geisha as in the Tokugawa period, or as a commodity as Uno did, is a violation of her human rights.

According to one journalist, Uno seems to have treated his mistress and her mother "in an egoistic, arrogant, and inhumane manner, revealing the least respectable kind of personality that people would expect of a national political leader." Uno's mistress agreed: "I think it is a serious problem that a man who makes a vulnerable old woman like my mother cry is our prime minister. Women do not care so much about money once we are in love."

What we have here is not a problem of women, but of the practice of prostitution. Many newspapers, however, have framed this incident as a women's issue, which is distorting and fallacious. Shimomura Michiko, a female reporter for *Asahi Shinbun*, observes:

Prime Minister Uno's scandal is regarded as a women's issue, because no distinction has been made between a commodified sexual relationship and a love relationship based on the free will of equal individuals.

On the one hand, prostitution is recognized as undesirable, but on the other hand, there is a trend toward sexual liberation. We have to be careful to distinguish between this incident and the issue of freedom in male-female relationships.

Uno's scandal is about the problem of prostitution, which is essentially a men's problem. The problem of men in Japanese society is symbolized by Prime Minister Uno's "least respectable kind of personality." The mass media, however, continue to write and pronounce this as a problem for women, not for men. While I am writing this commentary, TV news on the Upper House election results frequently cites "the women's problem" for the loss in popularity of the LDP. Again, let me articulate it correctly. As a Japanese social problem, this is a men's problem, and this incident involving a public figure, the current prime minister of Japan, is a manifestation of the problem of prostitution.

Indeed, Article 3 of the Anti-Prostitution Law declares that "no person should solicit or encourage prostitution." The woman solicited and Uno participated in prostitution. This is a fact. Uno committed a crime—he encouraged prostitution. Why shouldn't enraged women file law suits? Why shouldn't the police or the prosecutor's office take any action on this crime? Uno's mistress should be prepared to serve as a witness, since the incident has become well known. Uno should also be forced to testify as a suspect.

Incidentally, I wonder whether Prime Minister Uno, the suspect, understands that his role as the leader of Japan entails observing the laws of the land. The Convention on the Elimination of All Forms of Discrimination Against Women, which Japan ratified in 1985, prohibits prostitution. According to this provision, Prime Minister Uno must "take appropriate action" against himself, at least by resigning his position. Regardless of the result of the Upper House election, he should resign in order to amend for his violation of the Anti-Prostitution Law.

At the same time, I would like to encourage the woman not only to file a suit against Uno, but also to demand that the Anti-Prostitution Law be reformed. Under the present law the person who solicits is to be punished, but the party who "encourages" prostitution is free from punishment despite its illegality. This is a reflection of sexism. Of course, when a woman buys a man's services, it is the man who should be punished. In reality, however, it is mostly women who solicit and become criminals. This law, in short, embodies terrible discrimination against women. In the case of Uno, the prostitute's pursuit of justice would result in punishment only for herself.

Unfortunately, there are some women who do not understand the true meaning of this incident at all. For example, the actress Kaga Mariko said:

> I cannot stand that woman. She should not have complained about what happened. I don't mean to be prejudiced, but red-light districts are places to buy [a woman] or be bought [by men]. That's the way it is. I think that the classy way in which Japanese used to know how to play has declined.

Finally, I would urge women to pressure the mass media to treat the suspect Uno as involved not in a women's issue but in the problem of prostitution, which is a men's problem. If anyone continues to report on this incident as a women's problem, however, I cannot help but think that the reporter is trying to return Japan to feudalism by confusing prostitution with a voluntary love relationship.

1989

Anti-Internationalization: Internal and External Versions

A strange term, "internationalization," is popular; Japan is supposedly undergoing "internationalization." The reality, however, is different. In fact, Japan is in the process of being colonized while it is simultaneously reinvading other Asian countries. Increasingly, Japan has become culturally dependent on the United States, while Japan's attitudes to its neighboring Asian countries have become more and more disdainful, supported in part by Japan's economic superiority.

Internationalism in the true sense is a way of thinking or common understanding that works beyond national borders. Many Japanese, however, understand internationalism merely as being able to speak English.

The Japanese lack of internationalism is, as I have repeatedly argued, proved by the failure of Japan to assume responsibility for its part in the war and war crimes. Simply stated, the Japanese have no regret at all for the crime of aggression. In Australia, for example, the issue of war crimes is still discussed. Immediately after the media reported that a former

Australian air force officer would be tried for shooting 350 Japanese soldiers shipwrecked during World War II, the issue became a major topic of political debate in Australia. One executive at the state branch of the veterans' association commented:

> Why should an ex-soldier, one of our comrades, be accused of a war crime even though some Japanese war criminals have not yet been tried? I think that the bill on war criminals, which was submitted by the federal government and is now under review in the Senate, is really horrible.

This comment received applause at a party to celebrate the publication of a book on POW experiences under the Japanese military. Yet the media regarded this opinion as extreme. In my view, however, it is not extreme at all. The debate in Australia questions whether the victor should hold a trial of its own. Japan has, however, not tried Japanese war criminals (including the Emperor). The comment by the Australian veteran is empirically true and logical.

The Australian debate has not yet ended. But if we consider that war crimes can still become a significant national question, Australia looks much more international than Japan. The Japanese military massacred thousands of Chinese in Nanjing. The total number of massacred Chinese is estimated to be in the tens of thousands, which is much more than the 350 Japanese soldiers killed by the Australian air force officer. I am startled by the "anti-international" Japanese who ignore a much larger number of Chinese victims.

With such a flagrant manifestation of anti-internationalism, Japan is surely to be disdained and isolated by other nations. It is a crisis in which the survival of the nation is at stake. As a true patriot, I feel I need to warn the Japanese people. The question of Japanese war crimes has been revived frequently by neighboring countries. Unless Japan attains true internationalism, Japan's guilt for massacres at Nanjing and Malaysia, as well as countless other crimes, will be repeatedly put on stage.

Japan's anti-internationalism overseas is accompanied by anti-internationalism within Japan, particularly in regard to the problems of minorities. Japanese have not become internationalists in the eyes of Koreans in Japan and other peoples whose lands were invaded by Japan. Japan is startlingly insular and thus "backward." We should be concerned by Japan's xenophobic attitudes toward foreign students and workers from Asia and Africa.

The typical problem of minorities in Japan has been presented by the Ainu people. The Japanese invasion of Hokkaido was completed only about thirty years before the Japanese colonization of Taiwan. If Ainu had been stronger, Hokkaido would have become an independent Ainu Republic. In fact, soon after World War II, a discussion about implementing this idea took place. However, as in the case of Native Americans in the United States, because of the Realpolitik of population and military power, Hokkaido did not become an Ainu nation-state.

To be an Ainu in Japan is, however, very different from being a Native American in the United States. An examination of policies toward national minorities, not only in the United States but also in Canada, Sweden, Finland, and China, will demonstrate that the domestic version of Japan's chauvinism is as unique as its external version. Kayano Shigeru, director of the Nibutani Ainu Cultural Center, writes: "Is there any nation-state other than Japan that totally ignores the rights of indigenous peoples like the Ainu?" The Hokkaido Utari Association, an Ainu organization, has been working for the passage of a new law that would guarantee the rights of indigenous peoples, at least to the standard of other countries.

1988

Japan's Misfortune in Having Miyazawa as Prime Minister

Miyazawa Kiichi, who had long defended the so-called Peace Constitution, began to advocate sending the Self-Defense Force abroad in order to become prime minister. Around the time he became a pathetic "salaryman" prime minister,* many people expressed the following sentiment: "Since Mr. Miyazawa speaks English well, we can expect him to accomplish many things in foreign affairs. This is right for contemporary Japanese society, which is undergoing 'internationalization.'" Of course, it is better to speak English than not to speak English. This obvious assumption doesn't necessarily apply in all cases. Foreign reporters who can't speak a word of Japanese can nonetheless do excellent reporting by using a translator, while the converse—journalists who can speak Japanese but can't write decent articles—is not at all rare.

---

*The English word "salaryman" is used in Japan to denote white-collar workers.

215

Knowing English is one aspect of internationalization but not its essence. There are many Japanese who articulately express their isolationist sentiments in foreign languages. It would be better if these people remained silent in order to contribute to internationalism. An authentic approach to internationalism entails reforming people like Ishihara Shintarô who denies the existence of the Nanjing massacre.

It seems that Prime Minister Miyazawa is one of those who express nationalist sentiments in fluent English. Miyazawa was planning to transmit his speech to the 1992 UN Conference on Environment and Development in Rio de Janeiro by satellite. Right before the speech, UN Secretary-General Boutros Boutros-Ghali forbade the telecast. The reason for the cancellation was because "it would become a precedent." According to the *Sunday Mainichi,* some complained of the inequality between countries that can afford to transmit speeches and those that lack capital and technology. Others criticized Japan's arrogant attitude, saying that the Japanese believe they can solve everything with money.

These criticisms are justified in and of themselves. However, they are criticisms made by foreigners, who don't know much about the myopic nature of Japanese society. The immediate reason for refusal may have been lack of precedent, but the root cause is much deeper. In fact, this is where Miyazawa's anti-international attitudes most symbolically manifest themselves.

Most people have attended at least one funeral. At funerals, very few messages or telegrams are read. However, this Japanese custom has recently become quite popular. Messages are sent by people who should be at the funeral but are not. The message apologizes to the dead person and the immediate family for the sender's absence. Messages at funerals are like speeches. Moreover, the messages of those who are deemed famous and powerful are read first, demonstrating the disjunction between the traditional meaning of the message and its foolish contemporary manifestation. Thus rather than attending funerals, it becomes smarter to be absent and let those attending the funeral listen to one's speech. No wonder politicians have begun to abuse this custom.

This is what happened in Brazil. If it is not simply an ordinary funeral, but a meeting of world leaders, one can well imagine that it is a massive insult. It is not hard to fathom the anger of others who attended the Rio Summit.

In addition, Miyazawa's desire is a reflection of the Japanese avoidance of true dialogue. There are very few instances of dialogue between speakers and listeners, whether in classrooms, companies, or conferences. Although there may be a formal speech, the conclusion of the conference is usually decided by prior bargaining [*nemawashi*], and dialogue is all but meaningless. If one asks serious questions or advances perspectives deviating from the collective norm, one is bound to be excluded [*mura hachibu*]. Therefore, rather than engage in dialogue or debate, speakers can simply chatter. If that is the case, then why bother showing up—just send it by satellite. This peculiar Japanese assumption and logic is what Miyazawa tried to bring to Brazil.

What an insensitive and "anti-internationalist" sentiment! In spite of his fluent English, this chauvinist man is spreading shame around the world. It would be much better if he didn't speak any English. And what about Foreign Ministry personnel? Why didn't these "international" individuals try to stop the Prime Minister's "anti-international" and embarrassing

218 The Impoverished Spirit

activity? Were they, like Miyazawa, fluent foreign-language speakers and perpetrators of Japanocentric attitudes?

Miyazawa's provincialism is a reflection of a common Japanese behavioral pattern. We can see the characteristics of a myopic society in conferences without dialogue. Politicians who promote themselves are less international and sensitive than average Japanese citizens. I want non-Japanese people to know that average Japanese are not as insular as Miyazawa; this is an expression of my patriotism.

1992

Afterword:
A Manifesto
for Independent Journalism

I recently saw the movie *JFK*. What struck me most was the attitude of the U.S. mass media toward the prosecuting attorney, Jim Garrison—the relentless criticism by prestigious newspapers, journals, and broadcasting networks who defended the Washington establishment. It reminded me of Bungei Shunjū's twenty-year-old attack on my work—a series of exaggerations, distortions, and outright lies.

The mass media's connection to the powers that be is a frightful thing indeed. Given the tendency of power to corrupt, it is necessary for journalism to continue to criticize the powerful almost as a matter of course. There cannot be a coincidence of interests. In other words, if the mass media observes taboos it could be an industry but it would not be journalism. The U.S. mass media reporting of the Kennedy assassination was not journalism. One can also say that the Soviet Union did not have journalism; the same can be said for wartime Japan or Nazi Germany. How about Japan today?

There are no divisions of power in Japan today. I also argue that the fourth estate, journalism, which is supposed to watch over authority, has been corrupted. There are only a few courageous intellectuals who make radical criticisms of the status quo. Labor unions and students are also weak. Now, even our Constitution is in danger as the Self-Defense Force threatens to be dispatched abroad.

Japanese journalism has become an information industry for the status quo. Its rebirth, or *perestroika*, is not only unlikely, it is well-nigh impossible. Public broadcasting has become mere business. Newspapers have become cogs in larger conglomerates. True journalists are treated poorly, while sycophants are treated well. One would have thought that Japan was very different from the Soviet Union but because of its tadpole-like national character, Japan approaches the Soviet system of centralized power. The fact that *Asahi Jânaru*'s parent company, although it has other money-losing magazines, decided to end the publication of this journal is merely a necessary consequence of the policy pursued over the past ten years.

If it is impossible to be a journalist for the conglomerate newspapers, what can journalists, and others who desire true journalism, do? Is there any way out?

When judicial power has become a cog in the wheel of a centralized polity, it is impossible to establish another independent judicial branch. It would require a revolution to overthrow the country's power structure. However, freedom of the press is at least guaranteed by the Constitution, and, in fact, many new magazines are starting everyday. Since a daily is no different, the answer is simple: we should simply start a new daily that aims for true journalism.

In contrast to innumerable magazines, why hasn't a serious daily ever been published in postwar Japan? Undoubtedly, there are numerous economic and administrative difficulties. To the extent that a new venture must rely on corporations, it will be dependent on owners who threaten to turn a journalistic organ into a commercial one at any point.

Thus, in order to have a daily without restrictions, it is necessary to bring together free journalists, a newspaper that guarantees that freedom, and readers who demand such a newspaper. It does not have to be a large project, but it can't be narcissistically small or confined to a small region. Ideally, readers should overlap with editors and managers.

In other countries, there are recent successful examples: the *Independent* in England and *Hangyore Sinmun* in South Korea, which are both motivated by high ideals of journalism. In particular, *Hangyore Sinmun* approaches my idea of an unrestricted newspaper: to begin with, all readers are stockholders. Since readers supply the capital, it is not necessary to succumb to outside forces, such as corporations, political parties, or other pressure groups.

I have been discussing a new daily for sometime now—almost as a dream, indeed a joke. However, with the last issue of this journal [*Asahi Jânaru*], I want to introduce readers more concretely to this idea and request the readers' support and cooperation. I have been working with some colleagues along the following lines:

1. It will be a quality paper, to be published five times weekly.

2. Special issues on Saturday or Sunday will serve as a general weekly.

3. In principle, we will strive for home delivery.

4. We will establish managerial independence by asking all readers to become stockholders.

5. The editorial principle will be to eliminate restrictions and to be neutral regarding political parties. Thus, our "neutrality" is not the passive kind found in the existing mass media (eliminating "right" and "left"); we will be actively neutral, stressing environmental and human rights issues.

6. For routine news, we will rely on existing news services. All the staff writers will write signed pieces. We will begin by relying on veteran journalists.

7. We will revamp the organization and presentation of news materials.

8. We will introduce and report the findings of other newspapers and journals.

9. We will offer many pages to independent writers, photographers, and intellectuals.

10. We will attempt to collect information from abroad. In particular, we will stress voices from Asia and the third world.

11. Rather than just stressing novels, as in other newspapers, our cultural coverage will include music, drama, the visual arts, and so on.

12. We will network with various citizens' movements and report on their progress. We will also attempt to connect with foreign movements.

13. We will not merely list television and radio programs, but critically discuss them.

14. In order to establish the right of criticism in the mass media, we will emphasize critical perspectives and debates. We will fight against "mass media" pollution by offering our pages to people victimized by other papers and journals.

15. In the special Sunday (or Saturday) edition, we will include lengthy reports and essays. We will also include important speeches and reviews.

16. We will append many explanatory articles on important news items, providing necessary historical background.

17. We will respect the readers' (that is, the stockholders') opinions.

18. Although we will have advertisements, we will not be dependent on them.

19. Ten or so staff writers will constitute the editorial board and become the executive authority.

We are seeking stockholders. Once we have 50,000 stockholders, we will start publication.

Obviously, this idea is not my own. At this stage, several people are working together. Such a newspaper will brook no restrictions, and staff writers should be devoted to the idea of true journalism. In this sense, we are like a social movement, and we can be said to constitute a political party—hence, we can call ourselves the Journalists' Party.

*   *   *

With this final issue of *Asahi Jânaru,* "The Impoverished Spirit" comes to a close after 208 issues. This column has survived for so long in spite of internal and external pressures because of readers' support. I would like to sincerely thank those who have supported me over the years. It has been thirty-three years—the same thirty-three years that mark my career as a journalist and the life span of *Asahi Jânaru.*

"The Impoverished Spirit" began in the monthly *Ushio,* then moved to another monthly *Katei Gahô,* and then the current periodical. In the near future, it will resurface in a fourth journal.* Until then, farewell.

1992

---

*The column began appearing again in *Sunday Mainichi* in 1992.